C·O·N·F·I·D·E·N·T BEAUTY

C·O·N·F·I·D·E·N·T
BEAUTY

Reflecting the One Who Made You,
with the Images in your Mirror and in your Soul

CATRINA WELCH

Morgan James
Faith

New York

C·O·N·F·I·D·E·N·T BEAUTY

Reflecting the One Who Made You, with the Images in your Mirror and in your Soul

© 2014 CATRINA WELCH.

Published in New York, New York, by Morgan James Publishing. Morgan James and The Entrepreneurial Publisher are trademarks of Morgan James, LLC. www.MorganJamesPublishing.com

The Morgan James Speakers Group can bring authors to your live event. For more information or to book an event visit The Morgan James Speakers Group at www.TheMorganJamesSpeakersGroup.com.

BitLit
FOR ALL THE BOOKS YOU OWN

FREE eBook edition for your existing eReader with purchase

PRINT NAME ABOVE

For more information, instructions, restrictions, and to register your copy, go to **www.bitlit.ca/readers/register** or use your QR Reader to scan the barcode:

ISBN 978-1-61448-955-9 paperback
ISBN 978-1-61448-956-6 eBook
ISBN 978-1-61448-958-0 hard cover
Library of Congress Control Number:
2013949911

Cover Design by:
Rachel Lopez
www.r2cdesign.com

Interior Design by:
Bonnie Bushman
bonnie@caboodlegraphics.com

In an effort to support local communities, raise awareness and funds, Morgan James Publishing donates a percentage of all book sales for the life of each book to Habitat for Humanity Peninsula and Greater Williamsburg.

Get involved today, visit
www.MorganJamesBuilds.com

Habitat for Humanity
Peninsula and
Greater Williamsburg
Building Partner

DEDICATION

To my precious daughter, Victoria.

Your life has been an inspiration to mine, and a catalyst to my deep desire to understand the feminine heart. Watching you grow into a fine young lady who radiates confidence and beauty has been my reward, and ministering to women with you has been my great joy.

With all my love, I dedicate this book to you.

CONTENTS

Dedication   v

Preface   ix

Part One : The Spiritual Side of Confident Beauty   1
Supreme Makover
1. Barbie's Battle   3
2. Makeover vs. Made Over   7
3. The "More Than" Part of Skin Deep   13
4. The First Supreme MakeOver   *16*
5. The Great Pursuit   24
6. The Woman at the Well   29
7. Struggling with Vulnerability   33
8. My Own Struggle   42
9. Beauty in Balance   48
10. Insatiable Beauty   54
11. The Place of Balance   58

Part Two: The Physical Side of Confident Beauty   65
Your Personal Assessment
12. Confident Being Unique   67
13. Confident Being Imperfect   74
14. Rules of Confidence   81

15. Confident Colors   87
16. Confident With Your Physical Stature   96
17. Confident with your Clothing Personality   102

**Part Three: The Practical Side of Confident Beauty: 109
The Makeover**

18. Confident Classic   111
19. Confident Natural   119
20. Confident Dramatic   128
21. Confident Ingénue   138
22. Confident Romantic   145
23. Confident Gamine   154
24. Confident Knowing Your Personal Img.ID   161

About the Author   177

PREFACE

I remember the day I went with my brothers to get their hair cut at the home of one of my mom's friends. She was a professional cosmetologist with a concern for my family because we were in financial hardship. I couldn't keep my eyes off of her as I watched her perform the miracle of making even my brothers look handsome. I had seen my dad run the buzzers through their hair many times, but never before had I felt such a desire to do something anything. And so as soon as their hair started growing out, I begged them to let me try. I had my parents' support; after all it would save the expense. So at the age of eleven I set out on my life's ambition: to make people beautiful.

I was brought up in a Christian home, and my dad especially took the law of God seriously. He would often say things like, "If God wanted you to have curly hair, He would have given you curly hair." I always had and always will have a great love and respect for my father and so I didn't pursue the idea of becoming a professional cosmetologist. I also hid from him any attempts I made to look beautiful myself. I thought he would never approve of my career choice or of my makeup (which I would apply after leaving home each day), and really, his approval was all that mattered to me then.

So all throughout my high school years, I planned to be a tennis coach, like my mom. However, when I had assignments in my classes, such as job shadowing or developing a virtual business, I chose to shadow a hairdresser and to build a salon.

I continued my efforts to make people beautiful with my store-bought shears and began cutting the hair of anyone who would let me. I had a teacher who often gave me passes to return to the class I was missing while I cut the hair of her students and she watched. I also had the favor of a couple of the gym teachers who gave me their keys so that I could cut hair in the locker room.

I became well known as "the high school stylist," yet I had never had more training than that one visit watching my mom's friend. I was living my life's dream, although I never expected that I would ever get the formal training to make it a career, because I didn't want to offend my dad.

During my senior year I was the captain of my high school tennis team. Our team, including myself, was not very good. One day, I came home from yet another loss, and my dad asked me how it went. I told him the details of the match, and he responded with words that changed my life: "I think you would make a better hairdresser than you would a tennis coach."

To me it was as if he had said, "Permission granted! *Be who you want to be.*" I don't think a month passed before I was enrolled in Blaine Hair School and one thousand hours after starting there, I began my career as a cosmetologist at the age of eighteen.

I was barely twenty when I fell head over heels in love with a man and married him. They say love is blind. Well, I was completely blind to the things that should have been obvious, and ten days after discovering that we were about to start the family we were planning, he suddenly decided other women were more valuable to him than his commitment to me. Pregnant and alone, a war began to rage inside my soul. Some of my biggest battles were with self-confidence and how my beauty compared to the other women in his life.

People tell pregnant women they are beautiful. Friends who knew my story gave me plenty of affirmation, but I found it impossible to accept. Their words were kind but all I could hear shouting in my head was that I was a "throw-away-wife." When my status changed to "single mom" it only got harder, because the kind words were silenced. In our culture, compliments are for little girls and pregnant women; it's inappropriate to comment on a grown woman's beauty especially if she's a single mom!

On top of the longing to know I was beautiful, I often felt like I was being judged as a promiscuous fool for having a child without a man. Again, it wasn't so much the words that were said to me, but the ones I heard in my mind that were constantly attacking my confidence.

My focus was no longer on helping clients to look and feel good about themselves; instead I became obsessed with trying to look good myself. It was very hard to stand in front of a mirror all day and focus on others when my own reflection was screaming back at me that I wasn't worth keeping and loving. Some days were satisfying because I felt like perhaps I had proved my ex-husband foolish for giving me up for his new girl. But even on the good-hair-days the shameful reality that I had become vain and focused on myself restrained me from having any self-confidence.

I craved the attention and approval of others, yet I was never satisfied with any affirmations I did receive. Instead I only felt guilty for being a phony; every compliment only told me that I was a liar. I felt like I was fooling others with my professional skills, and that the truth was that I wasn't lovely at all. If I were, why would the man who promised to love me for better or worse throw me away?

It doesn't matter how kind and encouraging others are; our confidence comes from within and from above. I needed to hear from above that I was desirable before I could find it within.

It was during that time that I began seeking Biblical counsel and found the help I needed. I think sometimes we go through challenges in order to become better equipped to help the people around us. I began studying to be a Biblical Life Coach because I wanted to be better at helping my clients with their own "confidence conflicts". Women tend to pour out their heart when I touch their head (It just seems to be a beautiful benefit of being a hairdresser: they trust you with their image, they trust you with their deepest concerns.) I was always good at listening to their woes, but after my own experience I was far more understanding. Pain opens our eyes to the wounds of others.

Many years later, after finding a good, godly man and having a few more babies, I also furthered my education with certification in Image Consultation. Understanding the various types of feminine beauty revolutionized my life. As a cosmetologist we are taught to assess facial shapes so that the hairstyle balances and compliments our clients' best look and we are taught a little bit about skin undertones. But color analysis, facial features and the general style of the client isn't even considered, so gaining this knowledge certainly helped my career. It is amazing how much a woman changes when she understands what looks best on her and how to best accentuate her personal image identity (or what I call Img.ID).

Generally speaking, there are six Img.IDs (the Classic, the Natural, the Dramatic, the Ingénue, the Romantic and the Gamine) and many combinations of any two of them. Something very valuable happens to a woman when she gains the understanding of what her personal style is:

- Preparing for the day becomes much easier; so does shopping. Why? Because she knows which fashion trends and rules are important for her image and she no longer gets hung up on what not to wear. She lets other women enjoy the other aspects of hair, makeup, wardrobe and accessories that are simply "not her."
- She no longer compares herself to the other styles, and she begins to love and respect the differences in those whom she may have otherwise compared herself to.

And most of all:

- She can let go of all the hurts in her past that have hindered her from being her true self. Any confidence conflict is transformed into peaceful, confident beauty.

That is what happened to me. The other women in my ex-husband's life were not the only ones I compared myself to; my lack of confidence was the fruit of something deeper. Most women need to go back to their formative years and recognize where they got their understanding of feminine beauty.

My mother's Img.ID is Natural the casual beauty that truly feels fashion is foolish. The Natural radiates beauty far more in jeans than she does dressed up. I am a Dramatic. Not only do I love fashion, accessories and makeup; I need it all or my image is bland and boring. Once I understood that my mom was simply a different kind of beauty that I did not have to emulate, I was set free to be myself. I could respect her desires without disrespecting my own.

The change for me was so life-altering that I didn't want to use my new certification for just the professionals who could afford it; I wanted to help all my friends and clients as well as the women in my Bible Study. The more I consulted with women about their image the more I ended up ministering to them about the beauty battle within them. It has become apparent to me that there are common confidence conflicts and typical coping methods for each Img.ID. Knowledge is power; recognizing our thoughts and habits gives us the power to change what we need to and have grace for what we cannot. That's what creates true confidence and beauty.

Today my career and my ministry are one. My life's ambition is no longer just to make people beautiful, but also to help them know who they are. The most rewarding part of my job is to watch people become transformed into happier, more confident, energetic and motivated women and teens because they are less self-focused. I love to teach my friends and clients to care for themselves, so that they can forget about themselves and care for other people.

I have discovered that women usually find their identity in their relationships, and that often we are not confident in those relationships unless we are confident in our appearance. It is not easy to admit, but by nature we tend to believe that beautiful people are good, trustworthy, successful people, and we have an easier time accepting them. If we do not feel beautiful, we often feel unaccepted, un-ambitious and unwanted, and our relationships are affected.

We may jokingly call it a "bad hair day," but the truth is quite sobering: We tend to be grouchy and unapproachable when we do not feel lovely. Often we avoid people when we feel dumpy or ugly; we may even shun the people who catch us in such condition.

Have you ever run out of the house in your sweats with no makeup on and your hair a mess, when someone you know stops you to say hi? Can I guess that perhaps you did not take full advantage of that opportunity to build your relationship with that person?

When a woman is not confident in her appearance, she becomes self-conscious, and it is hard for her to think of others. Her mind tends to go to "I can't believe I've been caught looking like this," and that thought steals away her chance to encourage her friends because she is so wrapped up in herself. I've certainly experienced that!

Men think differently; they tend to find their identity in what they do. Their appearance isn't generally as big an issue for them, unless they are having trouble looking the part of their profession. Their wife's appearance, on the other hand, is also part of their identity, and it can be very important to them.

It all seems so shallow and meaningless, I know, to be concerned with our outer appearance. Most of us would agree that beauty is more than skin deep and it is the heart that matters, not our looks. Yet we can't deny that appearance is important to a woman, and that there are a lot of emotions attached to our image. I have found it is a big deal to us for a very real reason, and that there is an emotional battle raging within us because *it matters*.

I believe that each of us was created in the image of a mighty God who wants us to reflect Him, and that there is a trap set before us by the enemy of our souls that keeps us from being who God designed us to be. We need to know about that trap, and we need to understand ourselves and the battle within us if we are to be set free of the emotional struggle over our identity.

When a man or woman comes to that understanding, their paradigm is shifted and they become happier, more confident, energetic and motivated people. I have had women of all ages weep in my chair (I've even had a few men show a bit of emotion!) as I share with them what I want to share with you in this book. My hope is that you, too, will experience a paradigm shift that sets you free to be molded a bit more into the person God created you to be.

Reading this book won't stop the confidence conflicts from warring on your emotions any more than a highlight and waxing will. But I believe it will lead you to the One who will not only fight the conflicts with you, but will also bring you victory. After all, God is the Supreme Stylist, so to speak, who is able to give you what I call a "Supreme MakeOver" that will change you forever!

The concepts I will share are not complicated, and there is no prerequisite required to attain them. They do not cost you anything, and there is no "trap of maintenance" (like changing your hair color has!). The ideas and principles are simple, but getting to a place of truly understanding them may not come easily. But I believe you will find that it is a worthy battle. So put your armor on and get ready to fight for your identity.

If you are willing to put in the effort to grasp a hold of each chapter of this book, one concept at a time; if you are willing to search your soul; to take a good look at yourself; and to apply the appropriate pieces to your own life; you will be changed. The battle within you will no longer be the same. Your drive to have the approval of others or to have others be more like you will be defeated.

Most importantly, you will have a peace deep in your soul because you will know that you do not have to be someone other than who God created you to be; you will be free to be yourself, and to walk with confident beauty.

The story doesn't end with this revelation, however. This is not a feel-good book that you enjoy and put down wishing you knew what to do with all your new knowledge. In the second part of this book I will guide you in assessing your facial structure, figure frame, seasonal palette, personal preferences and clothing personality, and in the third part we will put it all together to determine your personal Img.ID. This final part includes many tricks of the beauty trade and much practical advice for how to accentuate your style and display your true identity, so that you can walk with confident beauty, which doesn't wear off like makeup does!

PART ONE

THE SPIRITUAL SIDE OF CONFIDENT BEAUTY:
Supreme Makover

*Because Beauty is
More Than Skin Deep*

CHAPTER ONE

BARBIE'S BATTLE

She was a beautiful woman. As she walked into the room with her head held high and her shoulders back, she caused all eyes to turn her way. Stunning. Her bouncy blonde hair framed her young, glowing face with all its perfect features so carefully made up. Her adorable outfit fit snuggly around her full figure a Barbie doll, that's what she reminded me of and she had the confidence of Barbie, too, I would have guessed.

Yet when I asked her, "Do you know who you are?" I was quite surprised at her response; I think you would have been, too. "I am a chubby, old, flat-chested brunette with a beak," she told me with seriousness that I didn't dare challenge.

There are many products and services available to enhance our beauty and change our body; many of them I offer in my salon. "Barbie" had taken advantage of almost all of them. She had had her hair bleached regularly since she was a teen, and she had learned back then how to carefully apply makeup and false eyelashes. She had been coming in weekly to have her nails done and monthly to have her hair cut and her face waxed. She had purchased products that helped her with her wrinkles and cellulite, and the circles under her eyes.

"Barbie" had also taken advantage of services I can't offer at my salon. With today's technology, the medical field can change nearly anything we do not like about our image. "Barbie" had had breast implants and nose surgery just after her divorce, and liposuction and laser treatments just after reaching forty. She looked good, and she knew it on the surface.

She could hold her head up high in a room of other women her age, but she struggled with the question: "Who are you?" She still saw herself with all the imperfections and shortcomings that she had worked so hard to alter. She had found no surgery, no product, no service available to treat the battle she fought within her.

The Bible says that "as a man (or woman) thinks in [her] heart, so is [s] he." Barbie fought a good fight on the outside. She was able to defy much of the aging process, but she had not changed her thinking.

She had grown up in a home that didn't seem to care for her. She always felt like she was in the way, a problem for those who were responsible for her. She seldom got attention unless she was alone with a man, and though the attention he gave never felt right, she desperately accepted whatever she could get.

As she grew up, she started understanding that it was only when she looked lovely that others noticed her. So dressing up and acting feminine became very important to her. She enjoyed the power she felt when others turned to look her way.

Making friends with other girls was hard, especially during her teenage years. They seemed to be threatened around her, but she shrugged off the pain of being disliked by them with the thrill she felt seeing them so intimidated. It was the only time in her life that she felt strong. And as much as she longed for true girlfriends, she didn't believe it was available to her.

Boys, on the other hand, seemed to flock to her. They would jump at her beck and call, and make complete fools of themselves on her behalf. She felt important to them. Her family had never even noticed she had needs, never mind jump to meet them. It was only around the boys that she felt like she was anything special.

She began to believe that it was for her beauty that she was valued. She longed to be noticed for who she was, not just how she looked, but her hope for that began to dwindle through the years.

There were times in her life that she decided her beauty caused more pain than it was worth. Like when girls despised her when they didn't even know her. She told me of times she had moved to a new area, and before she even had a chance to get to know anyone, they had made up their minds about who she was. They immediately decided she was "stuck up," because they assumed she believed she was too good for them. They wouldn't speak with her, but would taunt her and snub her, or simply look down when she tried to catch their eye.

Other times that her beauty became her thorn were when the boys would use her like a trophy. Over and over she would fall for their false interest in her, but, in the end, they really didn't care about her at all; they just wanted to impress each other with their "catch." To "score" was all they wanted, and she felt despised and used.

At times "Barbie" hated looking lovely, and she tried hiding her beauty in many ways. She found that if she pushed others away from her, they wouldn't have to push her away from them. So she tried making herself unapproachable; for a time, it was the extreme hair, then the "Goth" look that seemed to be effective. Later she intentionally gained weight wore frumpy clothes and let go of her hair and makeup to keep others at a distance. She actively sought rejection, so she could avoid the hurt of hoping for approval only to be disappointed.

The problem was, the more she played that game, the more she believed the lie that she was repulsive, and she began punishing herself for being so disgusting. She would starve herself until she became ravenous and couldn't help but binge when no one was looking; which, of course, made her feel guilty, so she would make herself throw it all up. She found herself fighting a huge battle, because her new habit became an addiction.

Although she was becoming seriously ill, the binging and purging gave her a false sense of control over the pain, and it gave her the strength to be vulnerable again.

But vulnerability, as we all know, only brings more pain.

"Barbie's" entire teenage years were back and forth: hiding her body with baggy, boyish outfits, then flaunting her figure with tight, revealing clothes; going without makeup, then layering it on heavily; hiding her face behind long bangs, then cutting her hair drastically.

She tried it all; striving to be beautiful, then hiding her beauty. Back and forth.

It was a very difficult time for her, as it is for many of us, while we try to discover who we are. We tend to test others with the shock-factor, until we find a response that we can live with, then we let that be the deciding factor on who we become.

By the time I met "Barbie," she had chosen to strive to look lovely at all times, no matter the cost. Her love for the power she felt when she knew she looked beautiful outweighed all the frustration she felt trying to be noticed any other way. Her decision made her one of my best patrons and one of my deepest burdens for ministry. I loved her business, but I felt her struggle. It broke my heart.

I see many, many "Barbies" in my salon. Women struggle with image. How we look reflects who we are, or at least whom we believe we are. We all fight a battle deep within our souls, often so deep that we have covered it up for years. But it is still there. We all long to be noticed; we all want to be lovely to someone.

Unfortunately, more often than not, that someone whose eye we've tried to catch hurts us, and we give up or we become obsessed with the challenge of striving even harder for the adoration we may never get.

This battle is being fought inside of every woman I have come to know. Don't get me wrong, I have been deceived into thinking certain women have somehow avoided this conflict, that "she has it all together." But after investing enough time into getting to know each of them, I have found no woman to be immune to the battle within. Therefore, I dare to assume that it wages war within you as well. In fact, it is why I am investing my time into this book.

I care about you, my reader and new friend, just as much as I care about "Barbie." I have fought this battle, too, and I want to help you fight it well, and so I ask you, "Do you know who you are?"

CHAPTER TWO

MAKEOVER VS. MADE OVER

The Supreme Difference

You are who you believe you are. When you do not know who you are, you will waver back and forth, just as Barbie did during her adolescence. When you believe a lie, you will be confused about who you are, just as Barbie is today, wearing the image of a beautiful woman, but seeing herself so completely differently, and speaking of herself so poorly.

Every time Barbie bought a product or had a service or surgery performed on her, she had a makeover she looked better, and she felt better. Often others would watch (makeovers are fun to see, aren't they?) and tell her she looked great, and that kept her going for awhile; makeovers are fun to have done. A makeover changes how we look and how we feel about ourselves.

When I am run down and not feeling well, I like to dress up. Most people dress for how they feel: when they feel run down, they put the sweat pants on or stay in their robe all day. I have found I feel better when I look better.

Think about how you feel when you are dressed up for a wedding. It isn't just the love in the air that makes a wedding so joyful. When you get ready for a wedding, you give yourself a "makeover" (or you go to a salon and have one done.) Makeovers make you feel good. I believe that most wedding guests are happy and "feeling the joy." simply because they feel good about themselves; they are looking their best and feeling confident about who they are.

I also believe that those who are not "feeling the joy" are feeling something quite the opposite. I have prepared many people for their wedding day or for their sister's or their girlfriend's wedding. Can I tell you that wedding-day-do's are the most difficult part of hairdressing, because that "battle within" is actively waging great war in the souls of those who are going to be standing before a crowd, and many cameras … the bride especially, and sometimes she puts the pressure on all of us servicing her. The term "Bridezilla" is no joke. It is not easy for most women to be the center of attention all day, having others gaze on her beauty. Preparing for such an event doesn't always bring out the best in us.

It's not just the attendants either; many wedding guests are challenged by the idea of being around so many people who are looking their best. I have never been to a wedding where every expected guest was there. I do not believe that the old "something suddenly came up" excuse is always the honest reason why there are so many empty seats. Wedding days run high in stress levels, for all who attend; and for those who do not know who they are, sometimes it is more than they can handle.

If you have ever felt anxious about the idea of attending a formal affair, please know you are not alone. I want to encourage you that after working through the ideas in this book, you will feel more confident in who you are, and choosing your attire for such an occasion could actually be a fun thing! You will know how to achieve "your look" and then let it go. You will be able to forget about yourself and focus on the people and the event.

My hope is that every reader will not only learn how to give herself a beautiful makeover, but that each will experience a "Supreme MakeOver."

What is the difference between a "makeover" and a "Supreme MakeOver"?

- A makeover changes how we look.
- A Supreme MakeOver changes who we are.
- A makeover changes how we feel about ourselves for today.
- A Supreme MakeOver changes what we believe about ourselves forever.

Before we can change what we believe about ourselves, we first have to take a good look at what we already believe. *Take a moment to really search your soul. I want you to think about the things that have touched you emotionally regarding your image (perhaps you have missed a wedding or two).*

- How do you feel when you have to stand before others?
- How do you feel in a room full of beautiful people?
- Have you ever surprised yourself with something you did or said that, after thinking about it, you now know was really all about how you felt about your image?

All you do and say, and even how you dress, comes down to what you believe. It is your **M**odus **O**perandi (MO), a Latin term for what really matters at the core of your soul, what drives you. There is a part, a signature aspect, of our MO that remains a constant and enduring part of each of us, (such as the desire to be lovely.) But our MO is a learned behavior that evolves over time as we gain experience in life. Each of us continually reshapes our MO to meet the demands of life and expectations (ours as well as others.)

In other words, we all want to be lovely to someone. As we experience life we make decisions about how we will meet that desire, or allow others to meet it, or we guard ourselves against ever trusting someone to meet that need again. Barbie's teen years are a great example of how a woman's MO can change as she experiences victories and defeats.

Barbie represents all of us women, but I would say her Img.ID (image identity) best represents a Romantic, the feminine beauty who tends to feel pain deeply. Her compassionate nature is what makes her such a great friend. She sincerely cares about others and is willing to sacrifice all she has to help them. Most Romantics are satisfied just knowing others appreciate all they give of themselves. They usually have a hard time giving to themselves, however, and they tend to either stuff down their own pain or look for someone to validate it. The Romantic's MO alternates between selflessness and selfishness, depending on what she is experiencing, and what her attitude is toward her circumstances.

The Classic, on the other hand, generally takes good care of herself. She is a proper and professional woman who knows what she needs to do to succeed in life and not much stops her from doing it. When it comes to her image, she doesn't give fashion a lot of thought. She knows the social standards and she lives up to them without becoming consumed by them. Each morning when she prepares for her day, a total makeover is part of it. She doesn't think about whether she will exercise and shower or not, nor does she think about finishing her look with shoes, accessories and makeup she just does it. She doesn't like to talk about it; to her it's a private matter and she really doesn't need anyone else's help or approval. Her alter ego tends to arise during chaos. When things go against her desires and convictions, or they become unorganized and out of her control, she tends to calmly shut down and dig her heels in until she gets her way.

Where a Classic feels makeup is a necessary evil, the Natural feels it is evil—or at least unnecessary—she's the casual girl who feels fashion is foolish. She doesn't really care much about how she looks or what people think of her; she is more concerned about being comfortable. This can be an issue if she has to go to a formal affair—her casual beauty can look (and feel!) awkward when she dresses up if she doesn't keep it simple. She may succumb to the stress of finding the appropriate attire and be the one who doesn't show at the wedding, but usually her faithful nature will conquer the stress, and she will cheerfully dress up and attend all the while wanting to be home in her sweats. This Img. ID is another one who has a hard time giving to herself. Although her selfless relatability is what makes her so beautiful, she needs to be careful not to let her beauty be swallowed up in the pride of being "real."

The Ingénue is another relatable beauty. She, too, makes others feel very comfortable around her because she is far more concerned about them than she is about herself… unless she has been hurt. The Ingénue who is raised by a loving and protective father and falls in love with a good man who will fight for her and her children becomes a powerfully beautiful and influential woman who lives a life that encourages others. This is not always the case, however. Because of the youthful nature and physique of this Img.ID, her beauty naturally calls forth a man's strength, and if he is not a good man he may treat her as an easy target to make him look strong. When mistreated, she can become bitter and hardened. Her tender nature is the most precious part of her beauty, and when her vulnerability is defiled her defense can be a strong determination either to take care of herself or to hurt herself. Either way, her delicate beauty is swallowed up in ugly pain. This Img. ID, like a delicate flower, doesn't need to strive for the attention beauty brings, but if it causes her hurt she may come to despise it, and if she has gotten to that place, she often remains there until she receives a healing of her heart.

There is another type of woman who tends to hide her vulnerability with a strong will the Gamine. This Img.ID, however, may hide no matter how she has been treated. She is bold, determined and un-intimidated by others. If anyone mistreats her, she has no problem setting the perpetrator straight. The Gamine's passion for life makes her fearfully fun: when she is happy, she is a whole lot of fun, but when she's angry she is not; people love her, or they fear her. She tends to be that way with her image, too. When she wants to dress up, her beauty comes alive, especially when she chooses bold colors. Unfortunately, her more favored look is quite casual and draining on her image and on her personality, and very often she is misunderstood because her image is saying one thing about her that her personality completely contradicts.

There is another Img.ID that is often misunderstood: the Dramatic. Her exotic appearance and passionate personality make her easy to remember and fun to be around, so popularity usually comes easily for her, but she needs to be careful not to get trapped by its insatiability. Dramatics have a way of going after what they want and if popularity is their drive, they tend to become the "drama queens" you see in the movies. Making friends is not her challenge, but keeping close friends is. She often has a sensitive nature and can be deeply hurt by friends who do not understand her or are intimidated by her drive and independence. When she is hurt, she only becomes more determined to be independent, and she withdraws from others.

Do you recognize yourself in any of these image identities?

Later in the book, I will help you assess your personal Img.ID and give you guidelines on how to best accentuate the beauty you were given so that you can be the best you in all your roles in life. But first you need to consider what you believe about yourself and how that belief affects your confidence in life.

You may have an immediate assessment of yourself, but consider if your answer is really yours, or is it the voice of someone you loved answering it for you? Does it reflect who you want to be, or who someone else wants you to be?

There is so much to discover about ourselves. But for the sake of keeping it simple, throughout this book we are going to thoroughly investigate who you are in your image. We are first going to look at why your image even matters, and if it's OK that it is so important to women to be seen as lovely.

Think about your answer again, does who you are have much to do with your appearance? How does your image play into what you believe about yourself?

What have you been taught to believe? Do you believe you are beautiful? Do you think it even matters?

Does the very topic of beauty bring up emotion in you?

I challenge you to press through those emotions and answer some more questions. Do not "waste your pain" by stuffing it or hiding it or ignoring it, but consider your emotions and why you may be feeling them.

Have you ever been rejected by someone because of how you look?

Has anyone ever taken advantage of you because of your appearance?

Do you find yourself trying to catch the eye of someone anyone even when you know you shouldn't care if they notice you or not?

Or do you find that you try to hide yourself, for fear of being noticed?

Have you ever put on weight just to keep a distance from those who hurt you?

Or do you repeatedly diet, striving to become more attractive?

Do you ever get frustrated that your husband didn't even notice your new dress or ... here's one I hear a lot: your haircut?

It can be hard to admit, but these things matter to us as women. You are not alone. And it is not wrong. It is part of who you are.

It matters because a woman's beauty is not only an *emotional* battle, it is a *spiritual one!* We are going to fight this battle together as you read this book. It may not be the easiest book to read (until you get to the practical chapters on the Makeover full of the "tricks of the trade") but not much worth fighting for is easy.

This is worth fighting for, and the victory is ahead. I am praying for you.

CHAPTER THREE

THE "MORE THAN" PART OF SKIN DEEP

Most of us believe in our heads that "beauty is more than skin deep." And I would dare say that many of us believe it in our hearts. But how many understand that **beauty is the very core of who we are ... and that is ok?** As an image consultant I believe *it is also skin deep* and I look forward to telling you which piece of makeup is most important for *you,* and whether or not to try something as bold as an extreme hairstyle ... but **there is something else that must come first: the "more than" part of skin deep beauty.**

First, I want you to experience that Supreme MakeOver; then the purely physical makeover will come easily. Remember, the Supreme MakeOver is done in the core of your soul; it is far more than skin deep. It is who you are.

To have a Supreme MakeOver you need to fight against all the emotions you have experienced in your past about your beauty emotions that the questions in the last chapter may have stirred up.

Perhaps you felt the battle of emotions as you read about "Barbie" in Chapter One. Did you relate to her in any way? If you felt it and are finding yourself defensive or doubting, or even angry or scared, I want to encourage you to press through those emotions. This is something that matters. I know it seems shallow or selfish, but hear me out: Stuffing or denying all the emotions we feel about the importance of looking beautiful is what our enemy wants us to do.

I know it's hard to think of beauty is an emotional battle, and that it seems far-fetched to think of it as a spiritual one. It is a difficult concept for most of us. In fact, even Christians are often surprised to realize which rival is on which side. But consider it well and store it deep in your heart: Satan hates a woman's beauty; God loves it and wants to use it for His glory. It is not the other way around.

Why is it such a big deal to our enemy? Because woman, not just man, was created in the image of God. And *woman is the reflection of the beauty of God.* The enemy of God is an enemy of you, my friend, simply because he is jealous of you.

Do you know that God loves a woman's beauty, like a mother loves her child? He does, because your beauty is a part of Him. I believe that it tears at His heart to see so many of us confused on the issue.

Proverbs 31:30 says that *"favor is deceitful, and beauty is vain, but a woman who fears the Lord, she shall be praised"* I memorized that scripture in my young Christian girls club, and grew up thinking the desire I had to be lovely was wrong, and that my Father in Heaven was ashamed of my selfishness, so I stuffed that desire and I hid my beauty. I thought that's what modesty was.

Others walk in arrogance of what God has given them and flaunt their beauty; they think it's all about them, and their pride hurts others. Many, like "Barbie," feel their beauty is their worth, and so they are never satisfied with it.

What are your beliefs about your appearance? Is there a scripture like the Proverb I knew that has formed your belief? My hope for you is that you will find total freedom and excitement in your understanding of this scripture and others like it before you turn the last pages of this book.

We cannot be truly changed, though, until we understand where we are at with our beliefs. Just as an alcoholic cannot change her ways until she admits she has a problem, so do we need to acknowledge what we are thinking about our beauty before we are set free to fight the battle within.

So let's take a look at what your understanding of beauty is now. Is it like most American women, who tend to think that:

- to be beautiful is to be vain?
- to be modest is to be "matronly"?
- a beautiful woman is a threat?
- an unsightly woman is invisible?

Satan wants to confuse you into believing you are *nothing without beauty* or that you are *cursed (to be used) because of it*. He loves to take the truth of God and distort it. He is an extremist. He forms his lies with one side of the truth, and then if we don't believe it, he takes the other side and blows it out of proportion and tries to convince us with that twisted-Truth.

Think about the see-saw Barbie rode: when she had no beauty, no one noticed her; when she worked hard to attain it, other women were threatened by her. They wrote her off as unapproachable before even getting to know her. When the men saw her beauty, they wanted her, but they put no value on her, just on the prize they would win. So she would go back to hiding herself...

It's all a trap. Don't fall for it. Do not fall for the lie that you must have a **perfect body to be anybody.** And if you have been blessed with beauty, don't fall for his lie that **that's all you are valued for!**

We are going to get into why Satan hates your beauty, and how God loves it when it is balanced. God is a God of balance, and I believe He longs to help each of us find the beautiful peace of a balanced life even in the area of image.

I will show you where I discovered these truths in the Word of God by showing you two Supreme MakeOvers, one in Genesis, one in John. That's right, the Word of God is the place to find all your answers to life, even on the issue of beauty. You might not find those "tricks of the trade" in the Word, but you will find everything you need for life and for godliness and you will find that beauty is part of godliness.

CHAPTER FOUR

THE FIRST SUPREME MAKEOVER

God created a world full of lovely creatures and plants, each with its unique design. Stripes and spots, smooth and thorny, patterns and textures, so much detail… He formed many landscapes and climates; the heavens with all their beauty and splendid sunsets and sunrises… all for our enjoyment. And isn't that what beauty brings? Enjoyment… peace… comfort… refreshment…

True beauty invites you to look a little longer, to understand it more to ask about its Designer. True beauty captivates you.

Remember, God not only cares about beauty, He loves it. He is beautiful and wants to be known for His beauty.

A woman's beauty is a reflection of her Designer. **God intended you to be like Him: beautiful, captivating, inviting, comforting.**

Your peaceful beauty is meant to be nurturing to others. For example, we know that pure beauty is healing; that is why we send flowers to the grieving heart. It is powerful. It is meant to inspire others to become better, stronger and more confident; that is why we vacation in beautiful resorts. Your beauty should bring peace, joy and energy to others. That is what Eve's beauty was all about.

Walk with me in the Garden of Eden; let me show you the first Supreme MakeOver. Notice I said *supreme* makeover; remember, this was not the kind of makeover we do in the salons, which would make Eve *look* different (although we do know she did get a new leather outfit!). This was the kind of makeover that *changed who she believed she was.* Unfortunately, this supreme makeover was not done by her Creator, but by her enemy…

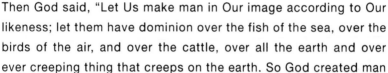

Then God said, "Let Us make man in Our image according to Our likeness; let them have dominion over the fish of the sea, over the birds of the air, and over the cattle, over all the earth and over ever creeping thing that creeps on the earth. So God created man in His own image; in the image of God He created him; male and female He created them. **Genesis 1:26, 27**

In Genesis 1, verses 26 and 27 (1:26-27) we see that Adam and Eve were created in the image of God—each one of them. Remember that God sees a married couple as one. Jesus Himself said that, "a man shall… be joined to his wife and the two shall become one flesh; that they are no longer two, but one flesh."

…He who made them at the beginning 'made them male and female'… for this reason a man shall leave his father and mother and be joined to his wife, and the two shall become one flesh… **Matthew 19:4, 5**

It is the one the union of the two different sexes that reflects the image of God. Think about that, God did not create man in His image and then create woman as an afterthought. He created man and woman together in His image.

Man is the image of the side of God that fights for us, pursues us, protects us, provides for us, and desires us, the powerful side of God that is a warrior…

Woman is the reflection of the gentle side of God that is relational, nurturing, comforting, encouraging, and responsive; the side of God that gives life and get this the side of God that longs to be sought after, longs to be seen for His (her) beauty. Let that sink deep into your soul. This battle within you, the core longing for beauty, is something God understands, something He put there to reflect Him!

Is that something you can believe?

It is not an easy concept to grasp, depending on what you have experienced in life. Many women I've met feel guilt and shame for their desire to be beautiful. Many of them do not tell anyone about their complex beauty routines, services or surgeries because they want others to think their beauty is "natural." The truth is, they don't want others to know that they long to be lovely.

We tend to look at each other and long for such natural beauty and yet we say "only her hairdresser knows for sure" and laugh, because laughter keeps the emotions more on the surface.

There was no battle within the feminine heart at the start of creation. Eve wasn't striving to be beautiful; she was a confident woman of God who knew who she was. She must have been; she walked around in that garden with her husband and Creator without a thought of her stark naked figure!

———— ❋ ❋ ❋ ————

And they were both naked, the man and his wife, and were not ashamed. **Genesis 2:25**

I love to say there are two kinds of women in the world: the kind who walks into the room and says "Here I am!" and the kind who walks in and says "Oh, there you are!"

I think Eve was the kind who didn't give a thought to herself. I can just imagine her walking through the garden and enjoying all the beautiful flowers and waterfalls, with all the birds and butterflies leading the way and the leopards and cheetahs brushing along her legs as she walked beside them. I imagine her and Adam sharing their hopes and dreams with their Lord as they were exploring all the landscapes and creatures that He had put before them.

——————— ❋ ❋ ❋ ———————

Then God saw everything that He had made, and indeed it was very good... **Genesis 1:31**

"Indeed it was very good." That is what God Himself said about His creation when He was done. This was His plan. Man and woman enjoying Him, enjoying each other and enjoying all that He had created for them. Free to rest and to play; free to adventure out together to discover all their hopes and dreams.

His creation was beautiful. True, pure beauty. Confident, inviting, comforting, peaceful beauty. Beauty that draws you to it and causes you to seek after the One Who created it. And Eve was the epitome of it all. That's what God's plan was for her to be. That's what God's plan is for you and me to be as women: a reflection of who He is.

Beautiful.

It all changed though, when Eve listened to the voice of another. There was someone who was jealous of who she was, and jealous of her beauty. Her enemy caused her to doubt who she was and made her start focusing on herself. (She became *self*-conscious!)

You know the story. Satan was a snake. He hated Eve. He hated them both, but it was Eve he came after because she was the beautiful one.

Remember, Satan left the throne of God where he had served as an "anointed cherub who covers," who was "'perfect in his ways from the day [he] was created, till iniquity was found in [him].'"

——————— ❋ ❋ ❋ ———————

"You were the anointed cherub who covers; I established you; You were on the holy mountain of God; You walked back and forth in the midst of fiery stones. You were perfect in your ways from the day you were created, till iniquity was found in you. **Ezekiel 28:14, 15**

He left God's side because he was jealous of God's splendor.

Ezekiel 28:17 says *"[Satan's] heart was lifted up because of [his] beauty; [he] corrupted [his] wisdom for the sake of splendor."* he wanted to be above God, and so God *"cast [him] down to the ground."*

Satan is not an ugly red creature with horns. He is a beautiful, clever, deceitful enemy of God … and of God's people the ones made in His image. He is your enemy.

--- ✳ 🐝 ✳ ---

...He was a murderer from the beginning, and does not stand in the truth, because there is no truth in him. When he speaks a lie, he speaks from his own resources, for he is a liar and the father of it. **John 8:44**

This enemy is known as the "father of lies." He can take a little bit of truth and twist it up with deceit and make things so confusing. That is what he did to Eve. The temptation he fed to her was not a delicious apple, it was the question, *"Do you know who you are?"* He was intentionally feeding her a lie (or a twisted-Truth) that she was not who God said she was, that God was holding out on her.

Look at how he confused her in Genesis 3:1: *"has God **indeed** said, 'you shall not eat of every tree of the garden'?"* (Do you ever feel him confusing you that way? "God doesn't want you to have *any* fun;" "Christians aren't allowed to do *anything*.")

Eve and her husband were only forbidden to eat of *one* of the many wonderful trees. God had blessed them abundantly with more than they could ever need or want, but He put one extra tree there in order to give them the opportunity to prove their love for Him by respecting His boundaries.

If they had no choice to disobey Him, then their relationship would have been a forced one. God wanted their love, proved by obedience, not just the company of two "robots" with no other option but to do as they were told.

Eve must have had a bit of the Gamine Img.ID in her because she wasn't afraid to correct Satan on this; she told him that God permitted them to eat from all the other trees.

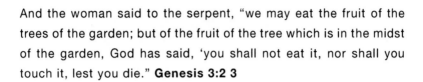

And the woman said to the serpent, "we may eat the fruit of the trees of the garden; but of the fruit of the tree which is in the midst of the garden, God has said, 'you shall not eat it, nor shall you touch it, lest you die." **Genesis 3:2 3**

Gamines have a passion for justice. If they see something broken they fix it, and they don't ask permission to do so. They are quick on their feet and full of ambition. Not much intimidates them and they don't understand when others hold back. I imagine Eve was like that.

She quickly accepted the seed of doubt, and she was thinking about her enemy's words maybe God *was* holding out on her. Then the sly one threw the big seed at her: "If you eat of that tree you will be *like God,* knowing good and evil."

Unfortunately, being quick on our feet is not always a good quality. Eve, like a lot of Gamines, formed an assumption about the goodness of God before really thinking through the facts.

Think about that.

First of all, Adam and Eve were *already like God!* ... And second of all, they *already knew good,* so really what Satan was offering them was the opportunity to know evil. What a snake!

What Eve was given was "indeed very good," but Satan made it look "shifty." He must have known she was a Gamine, and would act before thinking. Gamines are also very passionate about their convictions, and they tend to be very persuasive in making those around them agree with whatever they believe. I bet the snake knew that, too. He knew if he could convince Eve that God's law was unfair and that taking the fruit was right, she would convince her husband.

Not much has changed; the same enemy of God is still in the business of twisting up truth. And his MO hasn't changed either; he is still on a mission to destroy those created in the image of God, or at least to destroy their confidence in who they are!

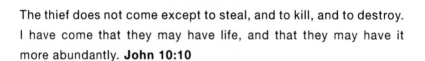

The thief does not come except to steal, and to kill, and to destroy. I have come that they may have life, and that they may have it more abundantly. **John 10:10**

And when it comes to women, he loves to direct his lies toward the issue of beauty. Your enemy knows that your image is an important part of who you are as a reflection of your Creator, and he hates the fact that you are beautiful. He will do anything to keep you from living your life as a beautiful, captivating woman of God who knows who she is.

Why? Because Satan knows just how powerful your beauty is. He knows which style of beauty you are and what your strengths and weaknesses are. Whether you believe it or not, he knows your image has the power to glorify God and to draw others to Him. And that is why he hates your beauty. That is why he wants you to hide it, hate it, or get hung up on it.

Eve decided to hide it. A lot of Gamines do. Look at Genesis 3:7-8:

Then the eyes of both of them were opened, and they knew that they were naked; and they sewed fig leaves together and made themselves coverings. And they heard the sound of the Lord God walking in the garden in the cool of the day, and Adam and his wife hid themselves from the presence of the Lord God among the trees of the garden.

They hid themselves from each other and from the presence of their Lord. Isn't that what shame does? It makes us pull away from each other, and from God.

Let me say it again: The temptation in the garden was not about Eve (or Adam) eating a piece of fruit. It was about them knowing who they are. The temptation is to be more, to know more; the trap is to be made to feel like a "nobody," and to pull away from everybody.

What happened that day in the Garden of Eden was a negative but supreme makeover. Eve was changed from the inside out. She started as an epitome of God's beauty, a true reflection of Him. She had peace in who she was. So much so, that she could walk around completely naked with total confidence.

She could share herself, all that she was, inside and out, with her Lord and her husband, with freedom and joy. But when she started doubting herself and her God, she suddenly saw herself differently: She found herself inadequate and shameful. She lost her confidence and the ease of intimacy.

Who she was, as a woman of God, changed; her eyes were opened and she knew she was naked. She was suddenly self-conscious, aware that she needed to cover herself up...and as a result all her relationships were changed.

Satan's makeover was successful (for him). Eve was a new woman: a fearful, self-conscious, unsatisfied woman in hiding. What she believed about herself had changed. She wasn't even conscious of her image before; now she believed she should hide herself from the ones who loved her.

Gamines do that, too. They are bold women who tend to see things as good or bad, and unfortunately they assume others see things the way they do. If they see in themselves something they don't like, they think everyone else sees it, too, and often they withdraw from friends who really love and respect them and wish they could be closer.

Thank God, Eve's story doesn't end with Satan's makeover—and neither does the Gamine's. God's love for us is stronger than our shame. Like Adam and Eve, we may make great effort to hide from God, but all our efforts do not keep Him from pursuing us.

CHAPTER FIVE

THE GREAT PURSUIT

Imagine Adam and Eve suddenly stunned to discover their nudity. I'm guessing that they stood there in shock, like a child who walks in on their mom or dad in the shower.

"Yikes! I saw you naked!"

Maybe they let out a yelp, as they each realized, "oh my, I'm naked too!" as they jumped into the nearest bushes. I can just picture them hustling around to find covering for their nudity before God returned for their evening walk. I wonder if their hands were shaking as they pulled off the leaves from the nearest fig tree and sewed them together.

But, hmmm, think how uncomfortable it must have been once the leaves dried out. Think how scratchy it felt. And the rustle of the dry leaves surely gave away where they were trying to hide from God!

Sounds foolish, doesn't it? We all know we can't hide from God. He knows what we are doing, what we are thinking and certainly where we are, but we still try, don't we?

I believe that God stood back and patiently waited while Adam and Eve ran around frantically attempting to cover their shame. God is a gentleman. He doesn't push Himself on anyone, certainly not when they are running from Him.

But He is also a Pursuer. He does not let his children hide forever. I can't imagine that Adam and Eve stayed in those bushes for long. I would guess that after they had their attire together, they came out into the open and did their best to act as if nothing had changed. Isn't that what you and I do when we are ashamed?

But then they heard the Lord God coming and they jumped back into the trees of the garden to hide themselves from His presence! We do that too, don't we?

———— ✳ 🌟 ✳ ————

And they heard the sound of the Lord God walking in the garden in the cool of the day, and Adam and his wife hid themselves from the presence of the Lord God among the trees of the garden. **Genesis 3:8**

It is uncomfortable when God is pursuing us; His presence confronts our shame so we hide even when we think we are ready to be found. But God doesn't give up that easily. He didn't give up on Adam and Eve.

———— ✳ 🌟 ✳ ————

Then the Lord God called to Adam and said to him, "Where are you? **Genesis 3:9"**

He called out for them because He wanted them to come to Himwith their shamejust as He wants you and me, no matter what we have done. He created each of us because He wants a relationship with us. Of course He wants us to prove our love with obedience, but just as Adam and Eve's failure did not change His love for them, His love for us remains strong as well.

We may fail to be obedient over and over, but the key is that we remain responsive. Adam and his wife responded. In Genesis 3:10 we see that they came out of their hiding and stood before the Great Creator and admitted: *"I was afraid, because I was naked; and I hid myself."*

They admitted their shame, which is a lot easier than admitting their sin; however, it is not enough. So God pursued them further, not because He didn't already know the answer to His question, but because they (and we) need to confess our sins, so that He can be faithful and just to forgive our sins and to cleanse us from all unrighteousness.

For years I thought Adam and Eve did a poor job at taking the responsibility for what they did; I thought their confession was simply blaming each other and the snake. After all, Adam did say, *"the woman whom you gave to be with me, she gave me of the tree, and I ate."* And Eve said, *"the serpent deceived me, and I ate."* (verses 12 and 13) It does sound like blame, and perhaps a bit of it was, but I wonder if God may have heard their heart say something more like this:

Adam: "You gave me this woman to be by my side, to walk together in obedience of the commandments you gave us, and I let her step out in front of me, and I listened to her instead of correcting her. I let her disobey you, and I didn't even speak up to help her overcome the temptation. Not only that, but I followed her and disobeyed you and ate of the only tree you told me not to eat of."

Eve: "I listened to the snake. I didn't resist him. I didn't consider your word, or your law; in fact I doubted who I am and your fairness toward me. I believed the snake's deception. I thought maybe you were holding out on me. I didn't even ask for Adam's counsel; I just grabbed at the fruit and ate it."

I believe their spoken confession was simple because simple is adequate. Sometimes we over-speak things; we need to remember that God knows the heart of our words. I believe Adam and Eve's hearts were right because God forgave them. Their confession, though imperfect, was enough for Him.

If you confess with your mouth the Lord Jesus and believe in your heart that God has raised Him from the dead, you will be saved. For with the heart one believes unto righteousness, and with the mouth confession is made unto salvation. **Romans 10:9, 10**

We could go into some deep theology here, but I am going to try to stay on our topic of a woman's image. After all, the trap set for Eve, remember, was that she wasn't who God said she was. Eve was created to be like God, yet she took it upon herself to try to become more like God.

God is a God of pure, peaceful, contented balance. His enemy is constantly trying to throw His people off-balance with greed, doubt and stress, so that He is not glorified. Satan's hope is that we would become obsessed and self-sufficient, or that we would become discouraged and despondent.

If we are successfully thrown off-balance, our focus becomes on ourselves and not each other or our Creator. That is what the snake wants! That is why he wants us to be embarrassed of our image or to get hung up on it. Because either way, we are only thinking of ourselves, and God is not glorified.

But consider how deeply God longs for us! Consider what He did for His children in the garden that day. He didn't come down on them for what they did. He didn't reiterate all that He had commanded and how they had failed. He simply dealt out the consequences of their behavior (the curse).

The consequences were blood, sweat and tears. To Adam He gave the sweat of hard work, and responsibility to provide for this woman. To Eve He gave the tears of the relationships in raising kids and always longing for her man, and having to submit to him.

And then came the blood.

...for Adam and his wife, the Lord God made tunics of skin, and clothed them. **Gen 3:21**

The Creator of the Earth made the great sacrifice of taking the life of one of His innocent creatures on behalf of the lives of His guilty children. Blood was shed for their sin, and the skin of an animal was made to cover their shame.

God chose not to force man (or woman) to love Him. But when they disappointed Him, He chose to love them anyway. He made them clothing that would not only respect their new desire to hide, but it was far superior to the leaves they had woven together and far more comfortable I am sure.

What a gracious God we have. He made for them sacrificial skin with soft textures. His outfit for them would far outlast anything they could have done for themselves. I am guessing that Eve's new coat was a beautiful, full-length mink or perhaps it was zebra's skin. I don't know, but I am confident that the colors and pattern God chose fit her seasonal palette and her spunky personality!

God fought to redeem Eve, and He is fighting for you. He wants His women dignified and unashamed of the beauty He gave us. It was not His plan that we should be covered, but because of our sin, we need to be. I know I do!

CHAPTER SIX

THE WOMAN
AT THE WELL

———— ❋ ❋ ❋ ————

He (Jesus) left Judea and departed again to Galilee. But He
needed to go through Samaria... Now Jacob's well was there.
Jesus therefore, being wearied from His journey, sat thus by the
well. It was about the sixth hour. A woman of Samaria came to
draw water. Jesus said to her, "Give Me a drink." **John 4:3,4,6,7**

We don't know her whole story, but there is much we can assume about
the Samaritan woman who underwent a Supreme MakeOver in the
gospel of John, chapter 4. She is known amongst Bible believers as the
"Woman at the Well."

I am going to call her "Samaritan Barbie" because I believe she may have been much like my friend in Chapter One, and that she, too represents all women. I assume that this woman had been striving for years to be seen as lovely, only to be repeatedly rejected and disappointed. The Bible says that she had had five husbands, and we see that she would rather go fetch her water at high noon than to get it with the others in the cool of the morning. It seems to me she found herself so ashamed that she could no longer face her peers.

Jesus made it clear in verse 4 that He *needed* to go where this woman was. When you look at the map, and know the culture, you realize that His "need" was not a navigational one. Samaria was not a good place for Jesus to be history tells us that the Jews and the Samaritans had a special hatred for one another, and going to their town was not only out of his way, but it was a dangerous place for Jesus to go which makes me think that His "need" was to rescue this dear woman. I believe she was nearly ready to give up on life.

I remember feeling that way when my first husband left me. Divorce is painful; I don't care if it is his fault or hers. God created husband and wife to be as one, and when the two are separated for any reason, it is like the shredding of two pieces of paper that had been glued together. Neither person is whole anymore, each of you has pieces of yourself missing, and part of the other still stuck on you. Divorce leaves you wounded.

I was enjoying a planned pregnancy, excited to start a family with a man I adored, when he suddenly surprised me with his betrayal. I know how painful it is to be a woman in love and discover that your husband loves another and has rejected you completely. The pain is … well, you can imagine, or perhaps you know, deeply devastating.

I lost hope to a degree I'd never experienced before. I believe God blessed me with the pregnancy to give me a reason to live, because I had thoughts that I wouldn't follow through on for the sake of the child within me.

———— ❋ ❋ ❋ ————

Be strong and of good courage, do not fear nor be afraid of them; for the Lord your God, He is the One who goes with you, He will not leave you nor forsake you. **Deuteronomy 31: 6**

I was divorced once. There were pieces of me torn off by just one other, and just one other man's wounds were left attached to who I was. I cannot imagine going through such turmoil repeatedly, like "Samaritan Barbie" did, without the knowledge that there is One who will never leave us nor forsake us. I got through that horrible time only by the grace of God. I cannot begin to imagine going through it five times!

I don't know what got this precious woman through her suffering over and over, but I do know she picked herself up and tried again and again and she was trying yet a sixth time to make a relationship work when she found Jesus waiting for her at the well. No wonder she came out of her home in the heat of the day, when everyone else in her village was staying out of the sun. After facing such heartache five times, she must have felt like she had no value at all. Most of us would have given up by then.

I remember feeling completely defeated during my divorce, yet I was desperate to prove myself still valuable; that's why I am guessing that the woman at the well was much like I was (and "Barbie"). I believe if she lived in our society, with all that is available to help us disguise our flaws, all the products and services that are so easily accessible to help us in our striving to be lovely, she would have the figure, attire and makeup of any super model we know.

I believe "Samaritan Barbie" must have looked her best, after all, she still had it in her to keep trying striving even to be lovely; because after five heartbreaks, she was in another relationship. She may have been hiding from other women, but she was still hoping a man could meet her needs.

I also believe that perhaps she was a Dramatic Img.ID because she obviously was a very determined woman. Dramatics have an exotic kind of beauty that can be threatening to other women. She may not recognize the tension her beauty causes but when she makes herself up (which she loves to do, and honestly needs to do, since her facial features tend to be washed away without makeup) she exudes a sense of confidence and power that is simply intimidating.

Dramatics usually are tall. Their height alone commands attention and, being a passionate person with a good work ethic, the Dramatic gives the impression that she's got her act together. While she is usually popular, she also can find herself left out of real relationships because of the assumption that she's all set and doesn't need anyone. Unfortunately, she tends to receive the assumptions as judgment or rejection.

It is naturally more comfortable for Dramatics to be with men, because they tend to accept her quickly and make her comfortable around them. Her private nature, though, makes her hard to figure out. Men may love having her by their side like a trophy but if they are not strong and determined themselves, they may give up on understanding her and walk out or detach emotionally from her.

The Dramatic's determined nature gives her the ability to keep going through the deep pain she feels from rejection. This may cause her to come across as aloof, but spend some time with her and you will realize that broken relationships can leave her wounded and feeling defeated.

No wonder Jesus was so desperate to rescue "Samaritan Barbie."

He knew that she desperately needed a Supreme MakeOver

Let's take a closer look.

CHAPTER SEVEN

STRUGGLING WITH VULNERABILITY

———— ❋ ❋ ❋ ————

A woman of Samaria came to draw water. Jesus said to her, "Give Me a drink." For His disciples had gone away into the city to buy food.

Then the woman of Samaria said to Him, "How is it that You, being a Jew, ask a drink from me, a Samaritan woman?" For Jews have no dealings with Samaritans.

Jesus answered and said to her, "If you knew the gift of God, and who it is who says to you, 'Give Me a drink,' you would have asked Him, and He would have given you living water."

The woman said to Him, "Sir, You have nothing to draw with, and the well is deep. Where then do You get that living water?

Are You greater than our father Jacob, who gave us the well, and drank from it himself, as well as his sons and his livestock?"

Jesus answered and said to her, "Whoever drinks of this water will thirst again, but whoever drinks of the water that I shall give him will never thirst. But the water that I shall give him will become in him a fountain of water springing up into everlasting life." **John 4:7-14**

When He arrived at the well, Jesus sent His disciples away to buy food for all of them, while He rested there because He was weary. (Notice Jesus was not afraid to have others help Him when He was in need … or to leave Him when He wanted privacy.)

Jesus knew "Samaritan Barbie" would be coming to the well at that hour. I believe He wanted to be alone with her, to help her through the struggles she was facing. Maybe you, too, have discovered that no matter how hard you try, no matter who you seek counsel from or try to talk things out with, you will never get the help you need until you take some quiet time alone with Jesus. When we need Him, He goes to that quiet, lonely place, and waits for us there, just as He did for this woman.

We learn in John 4, verses 7-14 how Jesus made Himself vulnerable to this defeated woman. How did He do that? He shared His own need with her … and asked for a drink.

The prejudices between the Jews and Samaritans at that time prohibited public conversation between the two, and especially between men and women. Jesus was making Himself very vulnerable, and He was asking a lot of this woman. Just speaking with Him went against everything she had ever known.

Remember, too, that Jesus was a rabbi, and a Jewish rabbi would rather go thirsty than violate these proprieties. But Jesus' love for this woman was far greater than any of man's laws or understandings.

Imagine how thirsty "Samaritan Barbie" must have been herself, and this Jewish man is asking her to not only talk to Him, but to serve Him the very thing she needed. When you are running on empty and others are adding to your workload, how do *you* respond?

The Samaritan woman's response to Him was defensive. It may have been fear and insecurity motivating her, or maybe it was conviction over the laws and prejudices she felt she was violating, but she actually stood up to Jesus and asked Him "how is it that You, being a Jew, ask a drink from me, a Samaritan woman?" Can't you just hear the question: *"don't you know who I am?"* Yet Jesus does not fight with her; instead, He offers himself to her.

"If you knew the gift of God and who it is who says to you, 'give Me a drink,' you would have asked Him, and He would have given you living water." Hear it again: *"Do you know who I am?"*

Often when God speaks in the physical, He is trying to reach us in the spiritual. Jesus offered her Living Water to satisfy her emotional and spiritual needs, but "Samaritan Barbie" doesn't understand what He is speaking about. She argues with Him that He can't help her: "Sir, you have nothing to draw with, and the well is deep. Where then do you get that living water?" Sometimes I feel that way, like my well my insecurity is so deep, my thirst so great, how could God ever meet my needs?

She also doubts who He is: "Are you greater than our father Jacob, who gave us this well, and drank from it himself, as well as his sons and his livestock?" It sounds like a ridiculous argument, when you know who He is, doesn't it? *Of course,* He is greater than her history; He created not only the well she speaks of; but the very source of its water He spoke into existence. Sometimes in our pride and need to figure things out, we forget who God is, and what He can do.

But Jesus was patient with her, just as He is with you and me. He simply, gently, reveals Himself to us. To "Samaritan Barbie" He said, "whoever drinks of this water will thirst again, but whoever drinks of the water that I shall give him will never thirst. But the water that I shall give him will become in him a fountain of water springing up into everlasting life"

Instead of fighting with her, or proving Himself, Jesus simply offers himself again. He knows what she is doing, how she is hiding. When He offers her water that quenches her need to ever come to the well again, He knows He is touching a sore spot and He knows she is not yet ready to receive what He has to give.

He wants to offer her hope, so He meets her where she is at, and reveals Himself little by little. He knows she is thinking about physical water, but His Word is a double-edged sword; it is spiritual water that He is offering.

————— ✳ 🌸 ✳ —————

For the word of God is living and powerful, and sharper than any two-edged sword, piercing even to the division of soul and spirit, and of joints and marrow, and is a discerner of the thoughts and intents of the heart. And there is no creature hidden from His sight, but all things are naked and open to the eyes of Him to whom we must give account. **Hebrews 4:12, 13**

Nevertheless, "Samaritan Barbie" likes His offer; she perceives that it would help her hide more easily if she didn't have to go to the well to get water every day. So she begins to open up to Jesus: "Sir, give me this water, that I may not thirst, nor come here to draw."

————— ✳ 🌸 ✳ —————

The woman said to Him, "Sir, give me this water, that I may not thirst, nor come here to draw."

Jesus said to her, "Go, call your husband, and come here."

The woman answered and said, "I have no husband."

Jesus said to her, "You have well said, 'I have no husband,' for you have had five husbands, and the one whom you now have is not your husband; in that you spoke truly." **John 4: 15-18**

Jesus is not satisfied with her response, because He knows she doesn't really understand, and He hasn't yet reached the core of the problem.

God wants to help us with how we feel about ourselves, but it isn't very often the easy way out... as my pastor often said, "He cares more about our character than our comfort."

Jesus didn't want to just help "Samaritan Barbie" become comfortable with herself by avoiding her fears. He wanted to heal her so that she could *look out not only for her own interests, but also for the interests of others." Philippians 2:4.* That is what He wants to do for each us; change our way of thinking so that it is not a surface makeover, but a supreme one that changes our confidence and belief in who we are.

Sometimes that takes looking at our history. That is what it took for this Samaritan woman; she needed to be healed of all the broken relationships that had left her shredded and torn like those pieces of paper that had been ripped apart. "Samaritan Barbie's" scars ran deep, so Jesus touched another sore spot, and asked her to "go, call your husband, and come here."

Someone once said, "nothing good in life ever comes easy." When God has worked in my life like He did in this woman, I have likened it to open heart surgery. I think there may be far more chambers in the heart than the four we learn about in biology, because I have experienced this kind of heart surgery many times; each time, God goes into a deeper chamber of my heart and removes another impurity.

We hide things deep in our soul; deep in our heart are things we have believed about ourselves that have made us who we are. Many of those things are wrong; whether they are pride or prejudices, or lies of the enemy. They need to be removed. It is a bittersweet experience to allow God to touch the sore spots in our hearts, take out His scalpel, and remove the old scars that have distorted who He wants us to be.

It is not easy, but it is good. We can trust God as the surgeon; the surgery may hurt, but He will never harm us.

It is hard to believe that God is for us, when so many have been against us. Which may be why "Samaritan Barbie" told Jesus she had no husband; she was hiding herself from Him. He hadn't won her trust yet. Jesus is patient; He knows this isn't easy. But He is also persistent; this surgery needs to be performed in order for the Supreme MakeOver to happen.

So He got out the scalpel and told her He knew her history. Listen to His gentle, encouraging words and see if you find any condemnation. "You have well said, 'I have no husband,' for you have had five husbands, and the one whom you now have is not your husband; in that you spoke truly."

God knows our sin; He knows where we have failed and who has failed us. We do not need to hide from Him; in fact, we cannot hide from Him. He knows our every thought, and all that we feel matters to Him.

In our self-defense we sometimes deny our feelings and try to avoid them, like this woman did. Some things just hurt so badly that we are better off not thinking about them. But just as a physical wound will only fester and grow infected if it is not cleaned out and dealt with, so will an emotional or spiritual wound.

Our Surgeon knows that; that is why He reminded "Samaritan Barbie" of her past. Sometimes we need to take a look back at our history. We certainly do not want to dwell there, but just as glancing in a rear-view mirror helps us on our road trips, so does glancing at our past help us to press on toward the goal of glory. We want to be sure there is nothing sneaking up on us, nothing demanding we slow down or pull over so urgent matters can be taken care of, but we must be cautious not to stare into the past, because there is great danger of crashing when we spend too much time looking backward.

———————— ❋ ❋ ❋ ————————

Not that I have already attained, or am already perfected; but I press on, that I may lay hold of that for which Christ Jesus has also laid hold of me. **Philippians 3:12**

There was an emergency vehicle sneaking up on this wounded woman. She needed to pull over, but her fear made her quickly change the subject. "Sir, I perceive that You are a prophet ... I have a question for *you* ..."

———————— ❋ ❋ ❋ ————————

The woman said to Him, "Sir, I perceive that You are a prophet. Our fathers worshiped on this mountain, and you Jews say that in Jerusalem is the place where one ought to worship."

Jesus said to her, "Woman, believe Me, the hour is coming when you will neither on this mountain, nor in Jerusalem, worship the Father. You worship what you do not know; we know what we worship, for salvation is of the Jews. But the hour is coming, and now is, when the true worshipers will worship the Father in spirit and truth; for the Father is seeking such to worship Him. God is Spirit, and those who worship Him must worship in spirit and truth."

The woman said to Him, "I know that Messiah is coming" (who is called Christ). "When He comes, He will tell us all things."

Jesus said to her, "I who speak to you am He." **John 4:19-26**

It is not easy to allow ourselves to be vulnerable. Aren't you glad our God is patient with us?

Jesus respectfully answered her question, and told her the salvation story. He gave her another invitation. He told her that she is wanted, that the Father is seeking true worshipers. When she responded with her hope of the coming Messiah to explain things to her, He told her, "I who speak to you am He."

Wow! Jesus didn't just straight-out tell people who He was. This was the first time He had said He was the Messiah, the One prophesied to come save His people, the One they were all waiting for.

He had bestowed an honor on this simple woman.

Take a look at how much that painful, but uncomplicated conversation changed "Samaritan Barbie." It was a "heart surgery" that performed a Supreme MakeOver.

Life changes when you know who Jesus is. Everything about you is different when you know you are wanted by the God of the universe.

———————— ❋ ❋ ❋ ————————

O Lord, You have searched me and known me, You know my sitting down and my rising up; You understand my thought afar off.

You comprehend my path and my lying down, And are acquainted with all my ways. For there is not a word on my tongue, But behold, O Lord, You know it altogether.

You have hedged me behind and before, and laid your hand upon me. Such knowledge is too wonderful for me; It is high, I cannot attain it.

Where can I go from Your Spirit? Or where can I flee from Your presence? ... How precious also are Your thoughts to me, O God! ...

Search me, O God, and know my heart; try me, and know my anxieties; and see if there is any wicked way in me, and lead me in the way everlasting. **Psalm 139**

Before this Divine appointment at the well, Barbie was walking wounded a woman in hiding. She avoided people and was concerned about herself and what others thought of her.

After meeting her Messiah, when the disciples returned and interrupted the conversation, she could have walked away, unchanged. But she did not. She could have grabbed the opportunity to return to hiding, but instead she left her water pot, went her way into the city, and said to the men, "Come, see a Man who told me all things that I ever did, could this be the Christ?"

She chose to believe the words of *her* Messiah, and to walk in that belief. She chose to become a true worshiper.

And at this point His disciples came, and they marveled that He talked with a woman; yet no one said, "What do You seek?" or, "Why are You talking with her?

The woman then left her waterpot, went her way into the city, and said to the men, "Come, see a Man who told me all things that I ever did. Could this be the Christ?" Then they went out of the city and came to Him. **John 4:27-30**

Do you see the supreme change? This woman was no longer concerned about what others thought of her. In fact she seems to have been totally set free of that. She knew her God sought after her, wanted her, fought for her and even forgave her. Other people's opinions just didn't define her any more.

She was now more concerned with sharing the Truth with others, than getting their approval. Look at how she left her old life, with all its fears and worries, and went straight to the very people she had been hiding from. She made herself vulnerable to the men of the city (just as Jesus did to her!). She became truly beautiful … a confident beauty!

And many of the Samaritans of that city believed in Him because of the word of he woman who testified, "He told me all that I ever did." **John 4:39**

Confident beauty is vulnerable, not concerned with appearance but rather with others.

Confident beauty is inviting. It calls others to come closer. It captures their attention and makes them curious, but it doesn't push itself onto others. It is modest and respectful.

"Samaritan Barbie" may have been *stunning* before, if I am right in my assumptions of her Dramatic, super-model approach to life. But she was not *beautiful*, until now. This was a Supreme MakeOver**,** because it changed who she was, not just how she looked!

This is what satisfies our Lord.

Remember that when Jesus sat by the well He was hungry and tired. Well, when the disciples wanted Him to eat, He told them, *"I have food to eat of which you do not know … My food is to do the will of Him who sent Me and to finish His work."* (verse 32, 34)

I believe the will of God is just this kind of change. He wants every one of us to be healed of the wounds we have suffered in our lives, and His desire to help us is so strong that it is a real *need* of His to go out of His way to rescue us.

Imagine the joy Jesus must have felt when "Samaritan Barbie" left Him to go face her fears, giving God glory and inviting others to Him.

Imagine the joy He feels when you do the same.

I believe God is seeking you out. He wants to do a Supreme MakeOver on you today. Are you willing to be vulnerable enough to let Him do that kind of "heart surgery" on you?

Because "Samaritan Barbie" was willing to be vulnerable, she was set free from hiding; her life was given a purpose bigger than herself. God was glorified in her, and many were saved.

CHAPTER EIGHT

MY OWN STRUGGLE

Let nothing be done through selfish ambition or conceit, but in lowliness of mind let each esteem others better than himself. Let each of you look out not only for his own interests, but also for the interest of others. **Philippians 2:3, 4**

Like Eve and "Samaritan Barbie" I, too, had a great struggle with vulnerability.

Recently, I discovered that I had sewn together some "fig leaves" of my own! I, like Eve, was hiding who I was. Only my fig leaves had the advantage of progressive technology. Some of my "leaves" were even digital! My PDA (Personal Digital Assistant … first a Palm Pilot, then my Blackberry, now an iPhone!) was hiding me well. I was BUSY.

I was constantly checking my task list and detailed schedule. I would almost panic if I was left to myself with free time because I didn't know which project to get busy on and hide away in. For me, busyness was a "fig leaf."

When I was a little girl, my enemy whispered in my ear that if I would silently suffer and quickly serve, God would approve of me; that was what I was created for. He told me that I am nothing unless I am serving others, and that others should not be bothered by my needs. Believing this twisted-Truth not only kept me from allowing anyone else to take care of me, but it kept me from being vulnerable to others in many ways.

I saw others' needs as my obligation, not as an opportunity to get involved in their lives, at least not on an intimate level, intimacy being a two-way street. Basically I would get involved enough to help, but I would not share my heart with them. I would hide myself from them in the busyness of caring for them.

Having been brought up in a Christian home and taught the word of God all my life, I knew God wanted me to look out for the interests of others. I had been trained well that way. But somehow, when I studied certain scriptures, like Philippians two, verse four, I missed the little words like "only" and "also." I thought it read "let each of you look out not … for his own interests, but … for the interests of others."

Now I see those two little words, and I understand that "not *only* for his own interest, but *also* for the interests of others" assumes that we do look out for ourselves, and that God *expects* us to care for ourselves. He *wants* us to. I hadn't grasped that part, until recently when I realized where I confused the concepts of respect, humility, submission and service. I had become legalistic in my approach to each of these things. I was living and breathing service and submission with an attitude of sacrifice. I had some close friends challenging me to slow down a little; they felt I was doing too much and that I was doing it all for the approval of other people.

I assured them that I was not doing this for accolades but I did seek God on the matter. In reality, I was after approval but not the approval of people. I was desperate for God's approval.

Growing up, I thought my service to others was my ticket to salvation.

My brothers were typical boys trying to prove their strength and they would often command me, "woman, go get me a drink." I would jump up and do it, not because I wanted to serve them, but because my precious dad once saw me do that and told me I was a good sister. I wanted him to smile at me like that again.

Looking back at that memory now as a grown woman, I am sure part of my dad's smile was a chuckle over his boys trying to be so tough, but it put an extra twist on what I began believing: that he approved of their command, and I shouldn't take their demeaning words too seriously.

Many decades later I was still believing a twisted-Truth: Jumping to serve others was respectful to God and to His people. It is. But God is more concerned about our heart than our actions, and He desires mercy and not sacrifice. We cannot properly respect others if we are not respecting ourselves; that is only false humility. Although I thought I was offering God a beautiful sacrifice, I was actually treating myself like a servant girl.

I needed to learn that believing that I am nothing and serving others for God's approval is not what He wants. (Perhaps your challenge is that you are looking for the approval of the one you serve, or your dad, or your boss?)

———————— ❋ ❋ ❋ ————————

For I desire mercy and not sacrifice, And the knowledge of God more than burnt offerings. Hosea 6:6

God does want us to serve others, but not because we are a "nobody," but because He is Somebody. He wants our service to be out of love for Him. He wants us to accept His love for us, not because of what we have done, but because of what He has done. Not because of who we are, but because of who He is.

Removing the leaves has not been easy for me. At first I felt great bitterness for all the years I had treated myself, and allowed others to treat me, as the "servant girl." I began feeling angry toward the ones I love, because I started to believe they saw me as a slave.

I wanted to rebel against my old nature and fight for myself and refuse to be the servant anymore. But I quickly realized I hated all those "poor me" feelings. I had to give it over, all the hurt, the resentment, the anger. It was too heavy, I couldn't hold onto it any longer. I would rather be "walked on" than be the bitter and rude person I was becoming.

I was overwhelmed trying to figure out how to handle my relationships now that I saw the Truth: *that I was just as valued by God as His other kids are.* Somehow it was just easier all my life to jump up and meet someone's need than to let mine be known.

I didn't know how to speak up for myself. I wanted to just stay away from others or keep hiding in my busyness. I was afraid to become vulnerable. But God showed me that He makes Himself vulnerable to us, and He sees our vulnerability as beautiful.

One day in worship I made myself vulnerable ... I laid it all down. I told God how sorry I was for believing so many lies for so long, for treating His girl (me!) with such disrespect, and for allowing others to treat me the same. I gave Him the shame of being such a fool, and the burden of dealing with those who had hurt me. And He gave me the strength to forgive them.

That time in worship was a battle, but when I finally did forgive, all the bitterness escaped my heart and my shame was erased. I was not released from serving others, but I was released from serving them out of shame for myself. I was free to serve God's people because of my love for Him, period; no more obligation, no more need of approval, just simple pure obedience out of love.

I became a new woman that day. I no longer jump to serve others because I am the "lowlife" who *should* do the work; I now jump with joy at the opportunity to *get* to do the work. I no longer feel ashamed of my own needs, but allow myself to be vulnerable, at least to the One who can meet those needs, and I am learning to risk being vulnerable to the people in my life that I can trust.

Not much has changed in my busy schedule, except that I have peace with it now, and I have freedom to not over-do, and to take care of myself. I used to resent that others didn't see my needs and jump to meet them like I do for them (even though I wouldn't even let them be known!). Now I understand that just as it is not always my responsibility to meet their needs, it is not their responsibility to meet mine.

I had believed that God liked me being a self-sacrificing silent servant, yet in all my serving I never found rest. I enjoyed making a difference in other's lives, but I was never at peace with who I was, not until my Supreme MakeOver, when Jesus spoke to me about what I was believing about myself.

He told me that He would love for me to still "esteem others better than myself" but that didn't mean I was of no value. I learned it is OK to care for myself.

Jesus did. He was humble and esteemed others; He made Himself a bondservant; He washed his friend's filthy feet. But He also took time out when

He needed it, even if others were demanding His time. And when He submitted to a horrible death for us, when He had nothing to be punished for, He didn't even open His mouth to defend Himself ... except when His enemies asked Him who He was!

But He kept silent and answered nothing. Again the high priest asked Him, saying to Him, "Are You the Christ, the Son of the Blessed?" Jesus said, "I am. And you will see the Son of Man sitting at the right hand of the Power, and coming with the clouds of heaven." Mark 14:61,62

Then Pilate asked Him, "Are You the King of the Jews?" He answered and said to him, "it is as you say." And the chief priests accused Him of many things, but He answered nothing. Mark 15: 2, 3

I think I could write another whole book on that topic, but for now just remember: **Jesus was confident about who He was** and He was not afraid to stand up for Himself, or to care for His own needs.

So I ask you, are you confident about yourself?

How do you try to hide who you are? Do you do like I did, and stay busy, giving to everyone but yourself? Or do you give up, thinking "it doesn't matter any way"? Do you avoid relationships, at least real ones, where you need to be vulnerable?

Most of us are hiding, each in our own way. Often we laugh and say "It's all good" and put on a movie or pick up a romance novel, or make a phone call. Sometimes we numb our pain with stimulants, or food, or exercise, or gossip.

Sometimes we wear baggy clothes or cut our hair really short to avoid any attention, especially from men. Other times we become desperate for attention, and we push others away with all our talking, taking and demanding.

Often we intimidate others with our obsession for perfection or beauty. We strive to look lovely, to appear valuable and wanted; but because we do not believe it and are not at peace about it, it makes others uncomfortable around us.

We need to become comfortable with who we are. I do not know any other way to achieve this than what worked for me. I had to spend that time in prayer and worship; I had to be alone with God and stay there until I heard from Him. I challenge you to go to the "well" and sit at the feet of Jesus for awhile and just ask Him how He sees you. Ask Him what He wants from you. Ask Him who He wants you to be

To do that you need to remove your "fig leaves" and allow yourself to be vulnerable to the One who created you. The things you are hiding behind are the things that are uncomfortable anyway (fig leaves dry out and become quite itching and scratchy....). God wants to put a coat of fur on you. Will you let Him?

You may need to be patient. It is not easy to wait while naked and vulnerable. But wait until He answers. Let Him speak, let Him put that mink on you, and when He does, write down what you are feeling, what you believe He has spoken to you.

Journaling may seem juvenile, but it is powerful and very helpful when the enemy comes to laugh at your new covering. He will. He may tell you it is foolish, or that it isn't even real. He may speak in a whisper when you are alone, or he may use a friend to speak it audibly to you. When he does, go back to your journal and stand on the words of your Savior. Stand on the words in belief of them, even if you do not feel lovely or loved. He said it, you are lovely to Him; believe it. He died for you, you are loved; accept it.

Consider your faith a gift to God and allow Him to renew your mind.

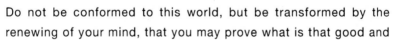

Do not be conformed to this world, but be transformed by the renewing of your mind, that you may prove what is that good and acceptable and perfect will of God. **Romans 12:2**

If you don't have a journal, write it down here:

CHAPTER NINE

BEAUTY IN BALANCE

God is a God of balance. He wants us to be a people of balance in all areas of our lives even in the area of beauty. When we walk in balance, we walk in great peace and joy. Our enemy is no fool, he knows that, and he does not want us walking in that place. He wants to throw our lives out of balance, so that we will be miserable and stressed out.

Satan is very good at throwing us off balance by distorting our understanding of the truth. He takes one side of the truth or the other and blows it out of proportion. When we believe these distorted truths we are left off balance and confused ... and God is not glorified in our stressed and striving lives.

The truth about beauty is that God designed it; He loves it, He wants it to reflect Him and to draw others to Him. He wants to be sought after for His beauty, and He made us to feel the same way.

Satan wants us to be ashamed of our beauty and to hide it ... or to seek after it with an ungodly obsession. We already took a look at how he had Eve trying to hide her beauty, ashamed of who she was. And then we saw how he had the woman at the well striving to be lovely, to be sought after, yet she was pushing away all her peers.

Both of these women were off-balance. They had each fallen for a distorted truth, (a twisted-Truth). Which side of the truth is the enemy of your soul blowing out of proportion for you? Is his attack on your beauty causing you to be ashamed of who you are? Or do you tend to idolize your desire to be beautiful? Have you given up on ever being lovely and do you walk in shame and self-contempt? Or have you determined in your heart that you will be lovely, no matter what the cost; do you believe that is how you are valued?

We all get thrown off balance at some point. There are a lot of powerful traps set to ensnare us with confidence conflicts. The bait is different for each Img.ID, though.

The Classic's desire to have things done properly can drive her to perfectionism and her true self may get hidden in busyness.

The Natural's desire for comfort may drive her to denial and her practical and unpretentious nature may get hidden in laziness.

The Dramatic's desire for popularity may drive her to demand attention to the point where it may swallow up her independent nature. Rejection and neglect may discourage her to the point of defeat.

The Ingénue's desire for peace may drive her to desperation or determination and self-reliance or codependency may engulf her beautiful complacent nature.

The Romantic's desire for acceptance may drive her to flaunt her beauty or focus on pleasing others and her compassionate nature may get swallowed up in selfishness or selflessness.

The Gamine's desire for justice may drive her to control others and herself so much that she may lose her fun, bubbly nature … and her friends.

For all of us, life is a continuous battle between shame and pride. It takes time to find the balance.

After nearly forty years of battling all my own emotions and shame about wanting to be lovely and after twenty years of hairdressing and passionately trying to help my clients feel beautiful, I became aware of God's heart on the matter, and His idea of "beauty in balance" set me free.

With a very graphic (and honestly quite confusing) metaphor in Ezekiel chapter 16, I discovered that there is a place of beauty in balance, and that when we are in that place, the God of Heaven is well pleased with us.

Well pleased. Not simply happy, but scripture actually uses the word "enthralled." I know it's hard to believe, after all the years of being mistreated for your beauty, or after being made to feel ashamed or selfish for wanting to be beautiful. It just seems far-fetched that a Holy God doesn't simply think its OK, but that He is actually enthralled by your beauty when it is in balance.

Listen, daughter, and pay careful attention: Forget your people and your father's house. Let the king be enthralled by your beauty; honor him, for he is your lord. **Psalm 45:10, 11 NIV**

Did you notice, the request in that verse? Let your Lord be enthralled by your beauty. Give Him that honor. The understanding of this truth, and that which is in Ezekiel 16, set me free—and I believe it will do the same for you. But don't take my word for it, read it yourself. It is God's Word that pierces our hearts and makes us new; my writing about it is not enough.

When you first read Ezekiel 16, you may find it quite offensive and hard to understand, because it gives some gory details about some very sensitive topics. Read it before you read my interpretation, or read it after, but I encourage you: read it, and consider what God says to you through it. His Word is not just history, and it is not just prophecy; it is alive and powerful for today ... and for you. Let's break it down together:

Again the word of the Lord came to me, saying, "Son of man, cause Jerusalem to know her abominations, and say, 'Thus says the Lord God to Jerusalem: "Your birth and your nativity are from the land of Canaan; your father was an Amorite and your mother a Hittite. As for your nativity, on the day you were born your navel cord was not cut, nor were you washed in water to cleanse you; you were not rubbed with salt nor wrapped in swaddling cloths. No eye pitied you, to do any of these things for you, to have compassion on you; but you were thrown out into the open field, when you yourself were loathed on the day you were born. **Ezekiel 16:1-5**

I believe that if you will truly take a look at this chapter in God's Holy Word, you will experience a Supreme MakeOver, and you will be set free to walk in that place of beauty in balance, free to be who He made you to be. The prophesy of Ezekiel 16 set me free from my emotional beauty battle, and I believe they could also be the words you are waiting to hear; it could be the "mink coat" He is wanting to cover you with. Don't forget to journal your thoughts.

In the first five verses God speaks of the heritage of His people; He makes it clear that He knows them (you) well. He has been watching you since you were conceived. God hand-picked your parents. He chose them to be the DNA pool from which you were formed.

My frame was not hidden from You, when I was made in secret, and skillfully wrought in the lowest parts of the earth. **Psalm 139:15**

You may have been a surprise to your Daddy, but you were not a surprise to your Heavenly Father. Even if you never knew your parents, even if you were the product of a rape, please know that you were not a mistake. It may have been a one-time union for your parents, but God allowed it, because there is no other way that you would be who you are if the two parts of your DNA had never united.

I believe God's perfect plan is that children are raised by two parents who love each other but because we live in a fallen world, and we are not robots who *have* to obey God's will, innocent people get hurt. And innocent children get abandoned by the very people who should have loved them most.

The metaphorical woman in Ezekiel 16 was left by her parents to die. She was a throwaway. No eye pitied her, no one took care of her, no one even cut her umbilical cord or cleaned her up when she was born. Before the modern day abortion, unwanted children were not destroyed within the womb; they were simply given birth to and then thrown out into an open field and left there alone to die.

Maybe you weren't abandoned so dramatically, but have you ever felt like that? Like no one cares, no one even knows you're there, no one is willing to help or listen, but instead you are despised and hated by the very ones who should be protecting and caring for you?

———————— ❋ ❋ ❋ ————————

"And when I passed by you and saw you struggling in your own blood, I said to you in your blood, 'Live!' Yes, I said to you in your blood, 'Live!' I made you thrive like a plant in the field; and you grew, matured, and became very beautiful. Your breasts were formed, your hair grew, but you were naked and bare.

"When I passed by you again and looked upon you, indeed your time was the time of love; so I spread My wing over you and covered your nakedness. Yes, I swore an oath to you and entered into a covenant with you, and you became Mine," says the Lord God.

"Then I washed you in water; yes, I thoroughly washed off your blood, and I anointed you with oil. I clothed you in embroidered cloth and gave you sandals of badger skin; I clothed you with fine linen and covered you with silk. I adorned you with ornaments, put bracelets on your wrists, and a chain on your neck. And I put a jewel in your nose, earrings in your ears, and a beautiful crown on your head. Thus you were adorned with gold and silver, and your clothing was of fine linen, silk, and embroidered cloth. You ate pastry of fine flour, honey, and oil. You were exceedingly beautiful, and succeeded to royalty. **Ezekiel 16:6-13**

I want to reassure you that God is the True Father, and that He cares. He is willing to listen and is able to help. Just as He was watching over this baby as she struggled in her natal blood and sustained her life when she had no idea He was there. In the same manner, He has sustained your life, even if you didn't know Him.

He may not force bad people to stop hurting you, and He may not make them do good things (because He has chosen to give them freedom of choice and He will not break His own Word), but He is able to sustain you, no matter how difficult life is.

And He is patient. Sometimes it takes us years to understand His love for us, just like it took this infant until puberty to notice her Savior; but when we are ready and willing to accept His help, He steps in and changes our lives.

And when we are ready, He gives us a Supreme MakeOver.

He took this girl to be His bride (and when you and I accept His love for us, He calls us the Bride of Christ). He made a covenant with her. Covenants are not contracts that end when one party quits or cheats or breaks the deal in any way. Covenants cannot be broken. If God's people should "break the deal," He is still faithful to His promises.

The God of the universe thoroughly washed this abandoned, unwanted girl with water, and anointed her with oil. Then, just like He did for Eve, He covered her nakedness! It wasn't with a fur coat this time; she must not have been a Gamine. Perhaps she was a Classic because instead, the Ezekiel woman was adorned with beautifully embroidered cloth of fine linen and silk. Her Savior even accessorized her with fine shoes, gorgeous jewelry, and a crown! God knew her Img.ID—a Classic needs to complete her look head to toe.

In verse 14, God says to His bride *"your fame went out among the nations because of your beauty, for it was perfect through My splendor which I had bestowed on you."*

Now that is perfect beauty.

Can't you just hear the pleasure in the Bridegroom's words? That's the place that I want to be; that is what I want for you, dear reader. Not necessarily the fame, not even the perfect beauty, but the approval, the sweet satisfaction in the voice of God speaking over you.

If I could paraphrase what I hear, it would be, *"I was so proud of you. You were the epitome of beauty. Everyone knew you because you drew them toward you with sweet, confident, powerful beauty. You were like Me, and you glorified Me with My splendor, which I had given to you."*

God wants you to become known for your beauty your confident, contented, "I know who I am" beauty. That is beauty in balance. It is not prideful or shameful. It is not selfish or intimidating. It is inviting. It glorifies your Creator. And it is His desire for you.

CHAPTER TEN

INSATIABLE BEAUTY

Imagine coming from the place of being despised and utterly rejected, to that powerful, peaceful, joyful place of beauty in balance. What a thrill it must have been to finally be wanted; others not only acknowledged her, but they were actually impressed by her! Before no one cared about her; now they desired her! She went from anonymity to fame.

We need to be careful though, because the enemy doesn't give up easily. This woman came from shame to a place of confidence, but she did not remain there. When we overcome one side of a twisted-Truth, the enemy tends to spin us around the other way, and our see-saw of understanding favors the other side of imbalance. Our confident beauty can become over-confident.

It did for this woman. Verse 15 says *"but you trusted in your own beauty, played the harlot because of your fame, and poured out your harlotry on everyone passing by who would have it."*

For the next 45 verses Ezekiel speaks for God of how disgusted He was in His bride's behavior. She had no respect for herself, for Him or for anything He had given her, not even their children. She got caught up in the awesome power that beauty brings.

We've seen it happen to many movie stars. We watch as their lives change when they get "discovered." They gain a little fame and start changing their image to "look the part"; they get noticed more and more and their confidence builds and builds until it takes control of their lives.

Remember, each of us has that core desire to be lovely, just like we all have the desire to eat … but if we only feed our bodies sugar (or caffeine, alcohol, drugs …) that is all our bodies crave. And the desire is insatiable, because it is not the substance we were designed to be satisfied with. It can become an obsession, or an addiction.

In the same way, if our soul is not fed the thing it was designed to be satisfied with beauty in balance then we, too, can become insatiable in our desire to attract attention. You have heard it said that you can be "addicted to love," but did you know you can be addicted to being desired?

I believe that's what happens to many movie stars; and I believe that's what happened to the woman in Ezekiel. I also believe it is what happens to every woman who gets caught up in the thrill of making others turn to look at her. When a man, in all his strength, is made weak because of a woman's appearance, she gets a high that can be just as addictive as any drug.

It *is* a thrill; can we just admit that?

The emotion is there from childhood. Every little girl wants her daddy to be captured by her; as she grows, she teases the boys to get their attention. But the older she gets, the desire to be desired becomes less innocent.

She begins to develop breasts and discovers a new power to make men weak, and if she is not trained well in how to handle that power, it can become a trap. We all know the form of a woman's body can be the bait of sin for man, but did you know it is a trap set to ensnare you as well?

When we fall into the trap that beauty brings because of its power, we change who we are.

Read through that section in verses 15 through 59 and notice how entrapped the Ezekiel woman got. Her first mistake was in sharing her beauty with anyone who walked by. It sounds so innocent, doesn't it? After all, beauty is meant to be shared, right? If it upset her husband, she must have been sharing too much of what was meant only for him.

The details in the written story are strong and graphic and may make most of us feel like "well, maybe I show a little too much cleavage now and then, but at least I'm not that bad." But I want you to see the heart of your Bridegroom on the matter.

Can you feel the hurt and horror in His words? *"…in all your abominations and acts of harlotry you did not remember the days of your youth, when you were naked and bare, struggling in your blood. Then it was so, after all your wickedness…you made your beauty to be abhorred. You offered yourself to everyone who passed by, and multiplied your acts of harlotry." Vss. 22-25*

I wonder how it started. I would imagine one day she simply got up the courage to wear that beautiful gown that she knew was a bit too revealing, and after the responses she got, she decided it was fun to show a little cleavage and watch the men's jaws drop.

Soon she not only gave away her body to be seen by others, but then to be had by them. Adultery is bad enough, and it doesn't satisfy. But soon, "Ezekiel Barbie" was putting herself out there like a prostitute, and then it got even worse; she still couldn't get enough, so she started *paying others to sleep with her!*

Imagine the heartbreak you feel when one of your growing children make foolish decisions, and they not only dishonor you but they end up getting used and mistreated. It tears your heart apart. You have hopes and dreams for them to do well all of their days, and yet you can only plan for them and guide them. You cannot control their lives; they must make their own choices.

God is perfect, and even His jealousy is perfect. This woman (and remember, she represents you and me just as much as she represents His chosen people of that day) was His creation, and she was not only unfaithful and dishonoring to Him, she was not only making foolish decisions that were causing her to be mistreated, but she was *asking* others to use her. She was *paying* others to take from her what God had given her for His glory. She was tearing His heart apart.

Verses 38 through 43 show us what the Righteous Creator/Husband/Father does next. *"I will judge you … I will also give you into their hand … I will make you cease … so I will lay to rest My fury toward you, and My jealousy shall depart from you. I will be quiet, and be angry no more. Because you did not remember the days of your youth, but agitated Me with all these things, surely I will also recompense your deeds on your own head."*

It is not a peaceful, joyful place when God steps back from the life we have chosen. It would be better to have His anger than His absence. He does not force Himself on His people. He does not make us choose righteousness. He is a Gentleman.

When we become stubborn and prideful, God steps back and waits until the time is right again to intervene, until we feel the consequences of our sin and return to Him. He is not a control freak, like we often are with each other.

The ending is beautiful, and we will get there, but first, let's go back to the place of beauty in balance. After all, that is where we want to be, right?

CHAPTER ELEVEN

THE PLACE OF BALANCE

L et's go back to that one verse in Ezekiel 16 that we only touched on. Verse 14 is the only verse that shows us balanced beauty. The first 13 verses are about God redeeming His bride from the lie that she was not valued, and verses 15-59 are about her insatiable desire to be desired. In one sentence God makes a powerful statement declaring His joy:

———————— ❊ ❊ ❊ ————————

"Your fame went out among the nations because of your beauty, for it was perfect through My splendor which I had bestowed on you."

Do you feel the pleasure in His words? God is pleased when our beauty shows His splendor. Beauty that is held back and ashamed of itself does not reflect God's beauty and beauty that is prideful and flaunting does not reflect

Him well either. But there is a perfect place that God approves of, and that's where the Ezekiel woman was for a short time. He approves of balanced beauty. What could be better? She was adored by her Husband who provided richly for her and she was loved by the nations. God's splendor, that's what He had bestowed on her; He said her beauty was perfect.

But apparently His approval is not enough for her.

In the very next verse His Bride's confidence is thrown off-balance and into pride. She trusts in her own beauty and takes on the "if you've got it, flaunt it" mentality.

I wonder how long she actually walked in the balance of confident beauty. It could have been years, I suppose, but there was simply not much to say about it. Think about that. Think about the women in your life that seem to have it all together. Are they women of many words? Is there much to say about them, or would you simply say, "wow"?

When we live a life of balance, our lives reflect the peace and joy of God. It is when life is off-balance that much is said. It's like the two little girls on the see-saw that weigh the same amount. When they are suspended in the air, in balance, they are simply smiling with glee. Yet to make that see-saw go up and down, there is more effort exerted, and they often let out a screech as their stomachs are pulled with the gravity.

In a sick sort of way, our lives may be more "exciting" when things are off-balance. But that is not joy. Joy is full of peace. When our beauty is in balance, there is not much to be said. We don't need to focus on our image (or others' beauty, for that matter) when we have confident beauty. Instead, we simply walk on, smiling with glee, because we know who, and Whose, we are.

I want that so badly for you, my new friend. I want you to be that little girl suspended in the air, just smiling with glee, talking with your girlfriend, without a care in the world in regard to your image. I want you to be able to enjoy life and bless others because you are not hung up on what you look like or what others think of you.

I believe you can have that. If you have come this far with me in this book, then you must be seeking God for what He wants for you. And His word says that if you seek, you will find. If you have not yet found the answers, keep seeking, and until you find them, be still and know that He is God.

——— ✳ ✳ ✳ ———

Ask, and it will be given to you; seek and you will find; knock, and it will be opened to you. For everyone who asks received, and he who seeks finds, and to him who knocks it will be opened. **Matthew 7:7**

Most of us learn like a girl on the see-saw. We take our new lesson to the extreme; we ride on the idea that beauty is vain, something to be ashamed of, then we ride the other side and believe that we are "all that" and thrive on the thrill of the power we find. It takes time to work out the balance. Do not beat yourself up if that is what you have done. Be encouraged by the ending of Ezekiel's metaphor.

——— ✳ ✳ ✳ ———

"Nevertheless I will remember My covenant with you ... Then you shall know that I am the Lord, that you may remember and be ashamed, and never open your mouth anymore because of your shame, when I provide you an atonement for all you have done" says the Lord God. **Ezekiel 16:60-63**

God is faithful, even when we are not. And He is persistent. He loves His girls, and He is willing to fight for us. He will keep His covenant with you even if you have broken your promises to Him ... even if you have "played the harlot" with all He has given you.

If you have confessed your sin to Him, then He has removed it from you and sees it no more. Do not speak of your shame as if it were still truth. Remember where you have come from (don't waste your pain, let it be used for others) but do not *live* it, do not *believe* it anymore. *It is no longer who you are*!

——— ✳ ✳ ✳ ———

Being confident of this very thing, that He who has begun a good work in you will complete it until the day of Jesus Christ. **Philippians 1:6**

Keeping beauty in balance is a challenge, but it can be done if we understand the truth, the truth that beauty is powerful.

It has the power to heal, to comfort, to encourage. That is why we send beautiful flowers to those grieving or depressed.

It has the power to captivate and draw you to it, to soothe you, and that is why we vacation in beautiful resorts, or take walks along the beach to unwind.

And it has the power to arouse; that is why men forget what they are doing or saying when a beautiful woman walks in.

The power of beauty is dangerous. The beauty of a woman's body has the power to destroy. In extreme terms, that danger manifests itself in pornography, so prevalent all around the world and growing in destructiveness. It can destroy man, and it can destroy woman, just as it did the woman in Ezekiel.

Beauty is not to be played with.

If we are to live a life of balanced beauty, we must respect the power that our beauty brings. We cannot use it to intimidate or tempt others.

Beauty in balance is modest. It is not true modesty to simply say, "I don't have that power" or "I don't think I'm beautiful or valuable." That is not modesty; in fact, that is twisted-Truth! Instead, a modest beauty knows her worth; she values herself and others, she is not ashamed to take care of herself (*not merely others*) and she is satisfied.

Each woman struggles to find the balance of having confidence with her beauty. It has been my experience that, generally speaking, each Img.ID approaches that balance in a similar way. Some women have a harder time than others, but balance seems to be a universal issue. Most women have confidence conflicts that tend to throw her off-balance, and all too often her image is the pivotal point.

So, how does each Img.ID come to grips with balancing these conflicts?

When the gentle, loving Ingénue is raised by a strong but compassionate father, her balance may come naturally. In fact, she may become the epitome of beauty in balance: she loves herself, takes responsibility for herself, and does the same for others within reason. People love to be around her because she cares for them, she sees their needs and desires and loves to bless them with her creative gifts. But she doesn't become overly concerned with issues that are not hers to control unless she falls prey to someone's manipulation of her generous heart and naive disposition. She has a youthful appearance and innocent nature, which naturally calls forth a man's strength. Good men will fight for her; bad men fight with her. An Ingénue who has been mistreated becomes like a wounded wolf: fierce and defensive and often deceitful. Her beauty gets thrown off-balance with either a determination to take care of herself, or with a desolate attitude of despair. Many wounded Ingénues fall prey to stimulants that numb their pain or habits that increase it such as cutting, or bulimia. Very often these are the women hiding under tattoos and piercings, subconsciously wanting to destroy their sweet, youthful appearance.

The Classic with a healthy upbringing tends to be well balanced in most areas of her life. By nature she is level headed and very calm, cool and collected, so she is less apt to get caught up in the emotions that the beauty battle arouses. She isn't ashamed to care for herself; she is generally regimented with her exercise program and eating habits and seldom becomes obsessed with image. She may get thrown off-balance if she lets her desire for perfection take precedence in her life. Her responsible nature does not want to be out of control of anything she is in charge of and if something comes into conflict with that, she may become intense in her efforts to regain a good reputation. Her driven nature may unconsciously push others away by making them feel inadequate around her, but in reality she is not as critical as they think she is. Really, she is just meticulous, but her beautiful, elegant nature is often hidden by her drive for dignity.

There is another calm, cool, collected Img.ID: the Natural. This woman does not care much about having things be proper, however. She is far more concerned with being comfortable; and she has a way of making others be comfortable around her, too. When she is confident and willing to share her simple beauty, she is very inspiring and inviting. She seldom gives in to the image pressures she may get from men, media and her mom. Heavy makeup and fancy attire only look phony or awkward on her casual and unpretentious nature. Perhaps that is why she tends to feel fashion is foolish. Her struggle with balance is usually more on the low side of the see-saw: it's taking care of herself that can be her challenge. She may be stuck on the ground with the weight of "being real," but she tends to think those high on the other side are stuck on themselves and she has no interest in being like them. Although people love this woman's carefree and faithful nature, unless she becomes confident about sharing her beauty (while keeping it simple and casual), she may make others uncomfortable with her apparent lack of concern for herself.

The Gamine is the like that, too: she would rather be comfortable than fashionable any day. She doesn't mind dressing up, as long as it is her idea, but she seldom gets hung up on image. Her beauty is thrown off-balance when her focus is. Gamines can be intensely driven; and although their focus is seldom for the acceptance of others, whatever drives them (usually their career) may overshadow their fun and encouraging nature, which is what makes them so attractive.

The other Img.IDs, the Romantic and the Dramatic, do tend to be driven by their desire for acceptance. These women may ride the see-saw of confidence conflicts a bit longer than others do before they find beauty in balance. The Romantic, like Barbie, and the Dramatic, like the woman at the well, may vacillate between shame and pride, striving for beauty and hiding from attention back and forth (or up and down) before finding the peaceful balance of confident beauty (which doesn't wear off like makeup does!).

It may take them (like most Img.IDs) awhile before they recognize their beauty or its power, but once they discover it, they may get caught up in the see-saw of confidence because these two types of women are passionate people who feel emotions deeply. When they are up, they are up; but when they are down, they are really down. Whether they are striving for attention or trying to remain out of sight, they are doing it with their whole heart.

When the Romantic is striving to be attractive, she may get off-balance with her sex appeal, with too much flirtatious makeup or overly revealing attire, making those around her feel uncomfortable with her immodesty, except of course, the men who want to take advantage of it. People may judge her as promiscuous, but her heart's desire may be naively to attract attention. Unfortunately, the attention she gets may lead her to deep pain, causing her to hate her beauty. Sadly, some Romantics experience being used by a man at a very young age (and often before she ever plays with the power her full figure brings). Her response to sexual abuse is to shut down and hide. She may do this with heavy makeup and more promiscuity (to punish herself, or to prove herself) or with extra weight or baggy clothes (to protect herself). Her efforts may be subconscious or they may be very purposeful, but either way despite how much this Img.ID cares about what others think of her, she doesn't think very much of herself.

The Dramatic tends to be a bit naïve as well. When she is striving for attention, she tends to do it with theatrics—and she may use fashion and makeup to make her statements, too, like they do in theater! Because of their passion to tell a story and their private nature otherwise, these women have a natural disposition to be trendsetters; but they can be rather ignorant to how difficult it is for others to keep up with them. They have a passion to have things look nice (their home, their kids, their selves!) but they somehow miss the idea that their drive for excellence may be intimidating to those around them. The way this girl tends to waver from balanced beauty is with her vulnerability. She loves to share her heart (if she has the floor) but because she plays up her story with her drama she often gets misunderstood, and she may vow never to share herself again … until her fervent nature pulls her back in to complete vulnerability once again.

While balanced beauty may be easier for some Img.IDs than it is for others, it never really comes easily. No one is excluded from needing healing for their hurts and humility for their haughtiness. Each one of us needs to work to find that balance.

Sometimes things happen in our lives that have nothing to do with which style we are; if something has rocked your see-saw, give yourself time to slow down the momentum of emotions. Remember, beauty in balance is not extreme. You will find a peaceful place of confidence and beauty that you can feel good about. Sometimes it's the life lessons that are most difficult that become the ones we understand the best, and end up helping someone else with.

That has been my experience.

———— ❋ ❋ ❋ ————

If anyone is in Christ, he is anew creation; old things have passed away; behold, all things have become new.
2 Corinthians 5:17

When we eat a proper diet, for example, our bodies are strong, healthy and full of energy; we are satisfied and not obsessed with our hunger. If we let go of our bad eating habits and addictions, we can walk in that place of "nutrition in balance" which is full of peace and joy. When we are hungry, we simply make ourselves a meal, enjoy it, and then not think about food again until our hunger returns.

We are going to get to that same place with your image. In the "makeover" part of this book we are going to talk about the proper "diet" for a healthy image. We will talk about how to prepare your personal look and let it go, not thinking about it again until you need to get dressed again. You will be able to enjoy who you are and how you look, and be satisfied.

I close this "Supreme MakeOver" portion of the book with this thought: Beauty in balance is a place of peace and joy, and it is attainable. It is Confident Beauty.

PART TWO

THE PHYSICAL SIDE OF CONFIDENT BEAUTY:
Your Personal Assessment

*Because Beauty is
Also Skin Deep*

CHAPTER TWELVE

CONFIDENT
BEING UNIQUE

So here you are: the new you. You have now experienced a Supreme MakeOver by the hand of God. (Forgive my assumption, but I'm assuming that if you have read this far, you have fought or at least are fighting the spiritual battles attached to beauty. I am assuming that God is doing an amazing work in your life; and you are beginning to walk in the victorious place of balanced beauty. I believe it, because I believe God answers prayer and I have been praying for you.

Now it is time to experience a makeover by your own hand.

You have learned that your beauty should not be something you focus your life on, nor should it be something you deny yourself and never consider a brilliant concept; but like any great philosophy in life, it is not truly great until it is applied personally.

How then do you apply this concept to your own life? How do you share yourself, and yet not get taken advantage of? How do you give of yourself and yet still find time to take care of yourself? How do you show your beauty, yet not flaunt it; or take pride in who you are, yet not become vain?

None of this is possible if we do not know we have a beauty to offer. If we believe that we have no real beauty of our own to offer that is *wanted,* our belief keeps us from offering at all. We hide. We think, "If you don't need me, I don't need to take the risk of offering something you may reject. Therefore I won't believe you need me."

Sometimes we simply don't want to believe we have a beauty to offer. It makes us too vulnerable. Yet vulnerability is the most beautiful part of woman.

In my experience, women have a hard time being vulnerable even to themselves! We don't want to be needy, we want to do things ourselves ... we may secretly (sometimes) wish someone else would just take care of us, but we can't handle the disappointment when they don't so we never ask, we just resent everyone else's neglect of us, and we either do what it takes (we strive!) or we give up on the whole idea of having our needs met.

When we let go of the disappointments and decide to take care of ourselves without the resentments, we can forget ourselves and focus on others. I want you to be able to let go of self-consciousness and be able to embrace "others'-consciousness." Talk about freedom! This is the main goal of my whole ministry. I want this for you, my friend.

I want you to feel free to care for yourself, and then free to no longer have to focus on yourself.

In order to do that you must understand your own needs and preferences; you must know how to manage them and you must appreciate others' needs and preferences, even if they differ from your own.

In order to appreciate the worth of another woman's beauty, we must understand that there are different types of beauty. We cannot enjoy our own image if we are always trying to compete with the images of other women.

We each have different personalities in character; we also have different personalities in image. Each of us has a unique beauty that was designed to reflect the glory of God, yet too often we get so hung up on comparing ourselves to each other that we put all our effort into trying to reflect someone else's image, and we do not reflect His image ... or show His glory at all.

In order to reflect the glory of God, we cannot get hung up on our own glory; and we must get over feeling as if we have no glory of our own.

We have all watched and lived the teenage years of trying to figure out who we are. It is an awkward time of trying on different characters that often just don't fit us well.

I remember trying to be fun and bubbly with my cheerleader friends only to be rejected for my phoniness. It was not that they didn't like my dry humor or contemplative nature, but that they didn't like me trying to be them ...

Perhaps you have been on the other side of that identity crisis, wishing your friend (or child) would just be who they are and stop trying to be someone they are not.

Sometimes it takes awhile to come to grips with the idea that we may not have the personality of the person we admire, but we are still valuable for who we are. It seems that it takes even longer to come to the same understanding about our image, especially for us women. Part of growing up is learning that life is not a competition and that we can admire people who are different from us, they are not a threat to who we are.

Being confident about who you are is key to escaping the trap of comparison.

Often, when I speak to groups of women about image, I bring a bouquet of flowers to illustrate the creativity of God. Each flower is unique, just as you and I are. Some are small and delicate; some are large and luscious. Some stand alone, others in clusters, but each individual adds something to the group. Here's how I see each Img.ID in relation to the bouquet:

- Classic is the Rose. Uniform, closed up when young, fragrant when mature.
- Natural is the Gerbera Daisy, carefree, casual, and unpretentious.
- Dramatic is a Bird of Paradise (the sophisticated Dramatic) or the Protea (the artistic Dramtic), long, lean, strong, and exotic.
- Ingénue is Baby's Breath, complimentary, enduring, and delicate.
- Romantic is the Orchid, glamorous, bodacious, and attention-grabbing.
- Gamine is the Calla Lilly, sharp, bold, colorful, strong and carefree.

Alone each flower would be beautiful; together they are even more so. When we look at a bouquet of flowers, we do not pick and choose which ones are most lovely. Instead we appreciate the diversity and splendor of the variety and contrasts.

We need to treat each other in that manner. It is not lovely when women become petty around each other. Far too easily we abandon the confidence we have in our own identity simply because another beautiful woman steps beside us.

When a petite and pretty woman walks into a room of strong and powerful women she tends to wish she were more exotic. Yet when the dynamic one walks up to the sweet, dainty one, she wishes she were more feminine.

We need to learn to appreciate one another's personal characteristics and respect our own.

Our Creator handpicked each gene when He formed us, He knew every one of our features would be the size and shape that they are; and it was not a surprise to Him. He chose your style, and mine, and He wants to be glorified in each of us.

The only way you can glorify God with your image is to learn and develop your personal style, so that you can best express who He created you to be. That sounds easy enough, but just as the girl in Ezekiel had to overcome her past, you too, need to move on from your hurts, in order to have that confidence that is so beautiful, no matter what image you were given.

Remember the words from Psalms 45:10,11; consider them your own personal Word from God:

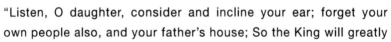

"Listen, O daughter, consider and incline your ear; forget your own people also, and your father's house; So the King will greatly desire your beauty; because He is your Lord worship Him"

It takes time to move on from all the emotions that are attached to our image as women. We need to allow ourselves time to heal and grow. Nothing good comes easy, but let me encourage you, that whenever you give over your fears, disappointments and frustrations to God, it is a sweet sacrifice of worship to Him; and He is well pleased.

I don't know about you, but the thought of God understanding and appreciating my sacrifice of pride and sufferings makes it all worth it to me! I have had to do this; in fact I still have to lay down my emotions including my fear of rejection, and my longings to be another kind of lovely quite often. But let me reassure you that when I give my Creator these feelings, He takes them and replaces them with confidence and compassion: confidence in who He made me to be, and in His love for me even with my flaws; and compassion for the ones I am envious of.

For years I resented that I was not given the full figure my mom has, yet my sister was blessed abundantly in that area; namely: the bosom. (She was also given my dad's beautiful blue eyes and blonde hair!) I never understood her when she would complain of the challenges her large endowment brought; in fact I only resented her more.

It wasn't until I gave my disappointments to God that I could hear her frustration through the noise of my own. My envy turned to compassion the day that I went with her to shop for bathing suits for her missions' trip. Suddenly I understood how hard it is for voluptuous bathers to look modest in our society.

When we only look through green (jealous) glasses we tend to see critically. (I was looking at my sister as if she was my opponent who was "putting it in my face" that I have not been as blessed as her.) Yet when we take off the jealousy, we not only begin to see the frustrations of the one we are threatened by, but we also see that our faults and imperfections aren't such a big deal. It is no longer a threat to you if the woman who has what you want is standing right beside you!

…or shopping right beside you, for that matter. After that day shopping with my precious little sister, I never hated shopping for my own bathing suits again.

There is something about every woman that she hates about herself—every woman. Sometimes it's obvious by the way some cower, and don't lift their heads, but even the ones who snub you and act as if they are "all that" are usually trying to hide their disappointments with themselves. We are each our own worst critics.

I have found that more often than not, it is the woman who looks most put together (the same one who you may consider to be a snob) who criticizes herself most harshly. Those trying to prove their beauty are often using the age-old trick of intimidation: they want to make their point before you take a good look at them and see the truth: that they feel the same way you do.

As if the beautiful women around us weren't enough of a test of confidence, we also have all around us the influence of media and market-driven idolization of certain types of beauty. In our culture, a woman's beauty is almost dehumanized. The pressure on the average woman to keep up with the cover girls and movie stars is sometimes more than we can handle. It is especially difficult not to let our imperfections become our obsessions or our depressions.

Seldom do we see any flaws on the models and movie stars we admire (unless they are pointed out in a gossip magazine; and then we tend to think it is a lie.) Why? Because they have professional help and technical support (and the power of computer programs like Photoshop and airbrushing) erasing their flaws and changing the angle of how we see them. We are left to feel like we are the only ones who fall short of perfection. That is not so.

We must remember: no figure is perfect.

Magazine editors and movie producers know how to use clothing textures, cuts and colors as well as hair and makeup techniques to correct most disproportions and imperfections with illusion (or Photoshop!). Image consultants and makeup artists get paid for what they do. Your payment may not be monetary (your pay will be your own satisfaction) but you don't need to be a professional to learn the illusions that create balance for your figure.

Let me give you an example of a teenage client I'll call Shelley, whose main challenge was her thick waist. Her mom had "concerns for Shelley's weight" which was interpreted by this girl as harsh criticism.

Shelley became obsessed with trying to look thin and beautiful, but her love for fashion and her misunderstandings of the illusions clothing lines create left her frustrated beyond what her young years could handle. She knew she had a thick waist, and her mom's disapproval of it had her desperate to hide it. She did not know, however, that the fashion trends that looked so good on her peers did not help her to hide her flaws.

Shelley loved to wear the popular multi-layered tank tops. It was fashionable to wear lighter tanks underneath darker ones, exposing the layers around the waist. The light line created by the layered tanks gave the straight figure of many of Shelley's friends the illusion of a beautiful curve. Shelley's waist, however, already had the curves, and the horizontal line only made her waist look wider; and the rolls of her belly became obvious. She thought she was looking sexy like her friends, but she was actually only drawing attention toward the very thing she was trying to hide.

Shelley, like most young women, could not see that good fashion for others is not necessarily good fashion for her. Drawing attention to her waist was not the best use of her "lines." She simply did not know what she was doing.

Shelley also liked to wear a thick, straight belt; she thought it would make her appear to have a thinner waist, but again, it only did the opposite: another horizontal line where she did not need width drawn, and another fashion trend good for her friend, awful for her.

This teen is not alone. Many women have this misunderstanding. Fashion is usually what leads our wardrobe; we tend to pick what's hot for the season, and don't even give much thought to whether it is "hot" on us or not. We need to realize that what works on the models may not work on us. We do not have to be slaves to the fashion industry. It is good to keep up with the times, but we need to be selective as to which fashion statements we put on our bodies.

Every woman has a personal style that is uniquely hers—that's why I like to call it her personal Image Identity; just as you can be identified by your fingerprint because it is your personal ID, it cannot be duplicated, your image is not something that can be imitated ... and neither can your girlfriend's, your favorite movie star, or the super model you adore.

It's time to be confident with who you are. Together we will figure out your personal Img.ID, including what your strengths and flaws are, then you will know where to draw the lines of illusion on your body, in order to draw attention to who you are and away from your imperfections.

CHAPTER THIRTEEN

CONFIDENT BEING IMPERFECT

Imperfections:

Before we go further to discuss how you can create those illusions, I would be remiss to neglect discussing figure flaws, or deformities that cannot be disguised.

Perhaps you have a birthmark on your face that no makeup can hide, or maybe you were only given one hand, or crossed eyes, crippled legs or very little hair. Maybe your beauty was taken from you by fire or injury or perhaps surgery-gone-bad. Maybe you feel as if you could never be beautiful to anyone ever; no matter how many tricks of the trade you learn.

I want you to know that if you were given a body that does not fit the moldone that does not meet the standard of beauty that is put in front of us day after day—but you are still lovely to the One who created you. That may sound appeasing or insensitive to say, but I know that it is true.

I know because I was blessed with a little girl of my own who had many deformities. Rebecca had twisted hips and crippled hands; her ears were low-set and rather bent and pointed and she couldn't shut her eyes completely. There were many imperfections in her precious little body, but she was so beautiful to me. It's true: it's part of being a mother, I know because I do the same thing with my other children: there is nothing more beautiful than the adoration a parent has for her child. I couldn't keep my eyes off any of my babies, but Rebecca was different.

Her beauty wouldn't have qualified her as a Gerber Baby, yet she captivated me, and all who looked at her, with her unique qualities. We all tend to adore beautiful babies, but when you hold a baby like my little girl, and see the peace on her face, it did not matter that some of her features were "flawed." Actually, in a way it was even more adorable.

I may sound biased, after all, she was mine, and beauty is in the eyes of the beholder; but I want to assure you that just as a new mother cannot keep her eyes off her baby, no matter the level of physical beauty, your Devine Designer looks over you so lovingly.

Your beauty has a purpose to draw others toward you, to reflect to them the heart of the One who made you. It does not require perfection. Just as the moon reflects the glory of the sun though it has many blotches, is far dimmer than the sun, and is even a different color, it brings forth light to the world. The moon is not bright and beautiful because of it's own glory, but because of the glory it reflects. A woman's beauty is the same way.

If you are drawing others to your Creator, you are beautiful!

I remember the day of Rebecca's dedication. During the service I was holding her tiny body in my arms just staring at her delicate deformities, completely in awe how different she was. As we began singing *"I sing for Joy at the works of your hands, forever I'll love you, forever I'll stand. Nothing compares to the promise I have in You"* I realized I was holding in my arms a great work of the hands of a Mighty God. This child was not a mistake; she was a special design of a very creative Father.

Rebecca was a Trisomy 18 baby; she had one more of chromosome number 18 than you and I have. That was why she had so many deformities (apparent ones, and ones unseen; including five major heart defects.) I do not believe that any of these irregularities came as a surprise to her Designer. I believe He chose each chromosome for her, just as He does for each of us. His Word says it, I believe it, and that is something that forever I will stand on.

Our baby was absolutely beautiful to me and to her daddy, and certainly to the One who created her. Please know that you are beautiful to your Father in Heaven too; no matter what your imperfections may be, compare them only to the promises you have in Him.

When others stare:

All that being said, it is still hard to deal with people staring at you. The stare of strangers is not as loving as the one of our Father. It hurts when the looks others send your way are so long and strong. It feels like you are under a microscope, like they are picking you apart.

Sometimes life seems unfair, but God is still faithful. Our understanding may be limited to our experience and our faith, but I believe that sometimes the unfairness of life is what increases our faith. Let me challenge you today, to see your life, your image, yourself, through the eyes of faith.

You were created to be beautiful. You may not see yourself as lovely; others may even have told you that you are not. But that is simply someone's opinion. Your Father in Heaven sees you as His masterpiece, and His opinion is the only one that holds any water. He is the One who gives you a purpose for living. He is the One who chose which genes you got from each of your parents. You are not a mistake even if you, like Rebecca, have "too many" genes and that has created problems.

Our bodies are temporary; there is a bigger picture. Whether you were born with an uncommon image, or it was a tragedy that robbed your beauty, consider that God has a plan in it all. He may not have wanted for you to suffer, but He allowed it, because He knew how He could work it in His purpose for your life. Remember, He allowed His Son to be rejected, abused and severely scared.

It broke God's heart to see Jesus suffer, but He allowed it, because there was a bigger purpose: to draw each of us toward His Father.

God is able to work all things to our good, if we give it to Him ... but again; it's still hard.

And we know that all things work together for good to those who love God, to those who are called according to His purpose. **Romans 8:28**

I remember when the doctors were trying to count Rebecca's fingers before she was born. They thought maybe she didn't have them all because she held them so tight and they overlapped. Rebecca was my first girl and I was looking forward to the day I would hold those hands in mine and give her her first manicure. But they were telling me that the number of digits she had was the least of my worries.

You don't hear of Trisomy 18 too often because most babies with this condition are aborted or stillborn; and those that do survive birth do not usually live longer than five days.

Rebecca lived three weeks before she passed away. During those three weeks, and the many, many long ones to follow, we had to wrestle out this stuff with God: Why is life unfair, and what do we do with all the people staring at us?

It wasn't just our daughter's uncommon beauty that people stared at.

Losing a child is out of the norm, and it makes people uncomfortable. Many times I've had conversations suddenly become awkward after I spoke of my loss; suddenly I became "different" to the one I was conversing with, and unless they had dealt with grief themselves, they no longer knew what to do or say around me; they stepped back and just stared.

Some things just don't make sense in life, and we just have to choose to trust God or not. It's not an easy decision, but I can tell you from experience that it is easier to give it all to Him than to become bitter toward Him. My husband and I figured out that if we could not trust God, there was no one we could trust, and we would be completely alone in our battle.

We chose to cast all our cares on Him, and He carried us through ... not that the battle is over, but He promises to give us strength to handle whatever comes our way. We look at it like this: If there were nothing "unfair" and we had no weaknesses or challenges, then our lives might be easier, but they would be empty and meaningless.

As they say, "nothing good in life comes easy." Having confidence in who you are and what your purpose is may not be easy, but it is good!

If you struggle with life being unfair to you, or you are tortured with thoughts about who you are or who you are not wrestle it out with God. Tell Him how you feel about it. Ask Him to help you deal with it. Perhaps that is the very purpose for Him allowing it: to draw you closer to Him.

He knows you better than you know yourself. Maybe He wants to use you the way He is using my husband and me. We have come to believe it is an honor and a privilege that others stare at us because of our loss. You see, if we were just like everyone else, no one would really get drawn to God by us.

Is there something about you that makes others stare at you? Let them look! And let God use you! I believe that is why He put your imperfection there; it captures others. Think about it: He trusts you to show His glory far more than the average girl who blends into the crowd.

Perfection and Jealousy:

It's not easy being different, and I have learned it's not easy for the beautiful girls either, because they get gawked at too, and not just by lustful men. They too get the long, strong stares and sometimes those stares can feel or even be threatening.

Sometimes the reason people stare is not because of your imperfections, but because they think you are perfect—or close to it. If God has shown His favor to you by blessing you with beauty, enjoy the opportunity to glorify Him well, but beware of what it can bring. We have already addressed it, but remember, there are two big traps set for you that can rob your peace and steal God's glory: your own pride, and others' jealousy.

There is something in every individual's life that can cause her to stumble over pride. We all have to remember that the gifts we are given are to bless others with, not to gloat over, just as others have gifts we need. Yes, your beauty is needed. It is needed to bring peace and refreshment and encouragement; if it becomes prideful it does not bring any of that to others. It is good to keep in mind that any unneeded gift can quickly be taken away.

Stumbling on jealousy is not as easy to recognize. You may notice the looks, you may feel the animosity, but you may not have any idea what is going on. The looks pretty girls get are not of pity, but of competition and envy, and who can contend with that? It is one thing to be hated or to have someone angry with you, even if it is unjustified; but to be the object of jealousy has got to be the most difficult place of all. I have sat with many beautiful girls who despise their beauty for this very reason. The big green monster (jealousy) has got to be the most difficult enemy to fight—maybe because he is so good at making you think you are the one who is guilty.

Beautiful women, no matter what Img.ID they are, suffer from the assumptions often put on them: that they "have it all together," that "they know they are beautiful" and are "stuck up" "promiscuous" or "showing off." They are sometimes despised for things they cannot change about themselves things that are not wrong.

Men and women both tend to think that a gorgeous girl is "above them"; it is often assumed that unless we too are gorgeous, we don't "qualify" to be friends with those more beautiful. When we are not confident with our beauty, we tend to think of beautiful people as unapproachable not because of what the pretty girls have done to make us feel that way, but because of what the enemy has done to make us feel that way.

If you are a gorgeous woman, and you haven't recognized this for what it is, and have only felt that false guilt and cynicism, you may feel very lonely. The hurt and rejection that beautiful women suffer often makes them cautious and defensive in their relationships.

You cannot change the way others feel, you must leave that with them; simply do your best to press through their judgments and show them the true you. My husband loves to say, "people of integrity expect to be believed, and when they are not, they let time prove them right." Give it time, pray that God would give you compassion for them and courage to keep being you despite their judgments.

The rejection jealousy brings cuts deep into your heart. I have ministered to women who have been wounded deeply by their friends, their sister or even their own mother who was jealous of them. Jealousy makes people mean. Jealousy brings forth hatred that hurts like few other violations especially when it comes from someone who should be on your side. I know no way to find victory over the jealousy monster in the world … it must be fought spiritually.

One of the most difficult parts of this battle is that in many ways it must be fought silently, since if you say someone is jealous of you, you come across as vain, and it seems quite judgmental of you, which makes you hypocritical since that is your accusation of them. This battle must be fought on your knees.

You really can't even deal upfront with the jealous person; you can't apologized for much since it is their emotions, and trying to talk it out (unless they repent of their feelings) doesn't usually get too far. When someone is jealous of your image, what can you do? You cannot change your height or figure frame, and why would you? Most likely they would still be jealous of something anyway!

Not So Average:

I have shared with you how I was the one wearing the big green outfit, shopping with my sister. Perhaps you have discovered that you are the jealous one in some of your relationships. It is hard not to let the fierceness of what we are feeling rule our life. But it is wrong to live our lives according to our emotions, especially if those emotions are hateful.

Funny, no one wants to be average, but we feel so robbed if we are below or above average in any way. We can't have it both ways. More than likely, you are not average in your appearance. Are you ready to accept that?

I had to take some time to wrestle this out with God. I had to let go of my false guilt over my desire to be lovely, and remember that my desire is a reflection of His desire to be lovely too. I had to talk to Him about my hopes and disappointments. I encourage you to take some time to do the same. Do not be ashamed to shed a tear with Him over this. Sometimes tears are the only way to be set free, because they are proof of letting go of control of the matter.

It is OK to grieve your loss no matter how big or small (sometimes our loss is simply the clear, smooth skin that used to be so beautiful and is now all wrinkled!) but don't do it alone. God longs to be your Comforter, and Friend, and these things are not too personal for Him. Give over to Him all that you feel about yourself, ask Him how He feels about you, and then wait and listen.

We must confess our sin, seek forgiveness, and choose to walk in truth from now on.

The truth is that you are enough. You were made in the image of a mighty, beautiful God. You may be imperfect, but you are a reflection of His glory. Let it shine, and let others see your beauty!

You are lovely in the eyes of the One who made you and His desire is toward you. Believe it. And let the truth set you free.

And then forgive yourself.

CHAPTER FOURTEEN

RULES OF CONFIDENCE

OK, so we admit it, we are imperfect, and sometimes people are just going to stare. But now what? We still need to fight this silly confidence battle within us.

We've tried the hiding, we've tried the striving, but in our hiding we are missing out, and in our striving we are hurting others. We have to find a way to fight that glorifies God, honors others and keeps us feeling good about ourselves. Is that possible?

You have heard it said, "if you can't beat 'em, join 'em." It's a saying that sums up the strategy I have found to be most productive in fighting this battle over beauty. Sometimes it all feels like a game, and we need to just jump in and play it. We all want to be lovely to someone; we all want others to look but not to stare. So let's just figure out how to look our best without being intimidating but remaining relatable, and then let's just do what we need to do so that we can forget about ourselves and think about life's bigger battles.

Know First Impressions Last:

Perhaps you have heard it said, "first impressions are lasting impressions." We make our first impression within the first six seconds of meeting someone new. It seems horribly judgmental I know, but it is a fact of life. You and I each sum up our opinion of others with the first impression they give us, and others decide if they like us or not within the first six seconds of meeting us. Granted, our opinions (and theirs) may change, but it will take some effort to make that change.

This is a major rule in the social standards of life. It is the first rule we must play by if we are to win this war on beauty. Our first and lasting impression is not all about our image; our voice, handshake, and body language are also factors others will subconsciously consider while deciding what they think of us.

Each of these factors stem from what we believe about who we are. If you believe you are of no value, then others will get the impression that you are of no value, and our Maker does not get much glory. If you have no idea who you are, or if you put a lot effort into trying to be someone else, then you will give the impression that you are a phony, and your Redeemer will be criticized.

Yet, when you believe you are "fearfully and wonderfully made" and you care for and respect yourself, then you give the impression that you are respectable, and God is glorified. If you believe you are precious to the King, and that the person you are meeting is precious to Him as well, then you give the impression that you are a humble princess, and others are drawn toward your Creator.

So what do you believe about yourself? (Go ahead, write it down, right here!)

What do you want others to believe about you? (Again, be bold; write it down!)

Know the Rule of Distraction:

Most likely you have been taught the proper edict of introduction: look the person you are meeting in the eye, hold your head up high, shake their hand with a firm, but gentle grip and clearly speak out "nice to meet you." This all says you are confident and it commands respectfor you, to them, and to the one introducing you.

For some reason not a lot is taught about image during introduction. Perhaps you were taught that your breath should be fresh and your face clean; but did you know that your outfit makes a huge part of your first impression?

Did anyone ever teach you that too much makeup can be a distraction to the person you are talking to (that is, unless you are a Dramatic clothing personality who can wear heavier makeup without it looking inappropriate)?

Did you know that if the colors you wear are not complimentary to your hair and skin tone, then they can be a distraction from who you really are?

Were you ever told that bold contrasting colors on a gentle, quiet girl will overshadow her, or that a girl with a Gamine clothing personality will come across as frumpy and boring if she does not wear bold contrasting colors?

Your attire says a lot about you. If your outfit says one thing about who you are, and you appear to be of another personality, the first impression you give may be confusing; it may even leave the subconscious impression that you cannot be trusted.

It is a petty and frustrating rule, I know; and I agree, it sounds quite confusing, but *it is important to dress within your personal image identity so that others don't look at what you are wearing and get a poor impression of who you are.*

This is the concept that sums up the rest of this book. You want your outfit, your hair and makeup to be *your look* (your Personal Image ID or Img.ID), so that no one really looks at your appearance. You want them to look at YOU.

You are found in your eyesthe "window of your soul." Your eyes tell others what you are feeling, and they tell others who you are. Your outfit, your makeup, your hair and even your accessories should always draw attention to your eyes; they should never take away from who you are.

Surely you know what it is like to converse with someone who is not paying attention to what you are saying. No doubt you also know what it is like to try to look someone in the eye and listen well to what they are saying, when they have something stuck between their teeth.

It is human nature to be easily distracted.

If we want others to look us in the eye and accept us for who we are, we must abide by the rule of distraction: *image, every aspect of it, should draw attention to the eyes.*

Know the Power of Modesty:

The rule of distraction is important for everyone, but especially for women. Why? Because a woman's body, not just her clothing, can be a distraction, and if the lines of her outfit draw attention to her figure more than her soul, she may find it hard to be known for who she is. It is not that a woman should hide her body but that she needs to understand the power her body has to steal attention away from who she is.

I was speaking on image at a teen retreat where the hostess showed a video that I will never forget. It was an interview of many teenage boys. Each of them was asked what he thought was an attractive girl. Most of them admired the not-so-modest fashions and admitted being drawn to the girls showing their curves and cleavage. When these young men were asked if they would date these kinds of girls, almost all of them said "oh, yes!"

The DVD continued, revealing more about these same boys and their ideas of their ideal girl. Individually, each one answered the next question: "would you marry that kind of girl?" Every one of them said "no!"

Women tend to see immodesty as a sign of strength; men see us as insecure when we think we must show what we have to offer without even being asked. They might enjoy it, but they do not want it for themselves.

In our culture, a woman's body, especially her cleavage, is the focal point of most fashions. Finding modest clothing is very difficult even for little girls. I recently went shopping for my daughter's first training bra, and it has become obvious to me that I am going to have as hard a time finding her something modest (or at least comfortable!) as I have finding her bathing suits every year.

Why is it that fleshy fashion is predominately all that is available?

Remember when we addressed the power of beauty? There is a counterfeit to this power: it is the power of showing feminine flesh. Immodesty is not only addictive, it is extremely dangerous for the see-er, and for the show-er.

This power was designed to be the most thrilling part of marriage, and it is only within the security of marriage that it satisfies for more than the moment. Anywhere else, showing too much flesh can destroy the respect each woman deserves. Men may desire the woman who shows herself, but only for a thrill; he does not respect her, and he leaves her feeling unrespectable.

Just as God gave woman the desire to be seen, He made man to want to see! They are visual creatures, and they like to fix things. Did you know that when a man is given part of a picture ... especially if it is of his greatest temptation: a woman's body ... he has an impulse to finish it? Look at the picture below. What do you see?

There is no triangle. There are three circles with a pie shape missing from each of them. Our minds are wired to fill in the missing part and complete the picture.

Vision is far less powerful to us than it is to a man. Just as your brain figured out that there was a triangle in the midst of those circles, so does a man's mind see beyond what is right in front of him, if you know what I mean. When a woman shows off a bit of what man wants to see, she loses her influence to sell what she's got ... he is already satisfied.

By nature, we respect things of value. If something is hidden, we value it. We want it more although we may grab at things available, (like those boys interviewed: they wanted the immodest girls as trophies, but did not value them enough to be their wife.)

In marketing, what is referred to as the "curiosity approach" is one of the most effective techniques of raising sales. This approach is also what is most effective in attracting a man. If you want someone to desire what you have, you must give only a taste, so that they want more. If you show too much of your body, you take away the power of curiosity. Modesty creates true desire, not just lust, because its mystery creates curiosity and commands respect.

I heard one man compare the immodest woman to fireworks: "she may draw us to look, but we see what we want, then we quickly forget her, because we are not truly satisfied." Yet a modest woman he described as "a candle that captures man's gaze and invites him to relax around her."

As God's girls, we need to value what we have to offer, and not show it off to anyone passing by.

As godly wives we need not hide our bodies from the man we promised to give ourselves to (in our husband's bed the power we were given is safe to enjoy) but we must be careful not to fall for the counterfeit power of showing our stuff to other men. The question is: Is it more powerful to cause a man to look your way or to have his respect and admiration?

Modesty is the true power of a woman's beauty. It's power is in the mystery.

Maybe you are not proud of your body and are not intending to show it off, yet you face this modesty issue every day because you have been well endowed with curves you cannot hide. We are going to address that be sure to read the section on the Romantic Clothing Personality.

For right now, realize that the focus shouldn't be on your body; whether because of your choices or because of your challenges, the focus should be on who you are.

This can happen for you if you know how to draw the eye of your onlooker into the window of your soul. When others look into your eyes their first impression of you will be a glimpse of who you truly are. That is when you will have Confident Beauty, and others will have confidence in you.

CHAPTER FIFTEEN

CONFIDENT COLORS

The largest factor in making a good first impression with your image is color. The colors you choose for your hair, skin, nails and attire say a lot about who you are for two reasons. First, because the colors you wear cause your skin tone to respond either to your advantage or to your disadvantage. Secondly, because color has a huge effect on human emotions, and the colors you choose are speaking not only to the person you are meeting, but you too may be subconsciously responding to them.

It is to your benefit to understand your colors.

Color should compliment skin tone, harmonize with the undertones in your hair, skin and eyes, and enlarge and brighten the eyes, lifting the face.

Know which colors draw attention to your eyes.
Only purchase colors that suit you best.

Know the Physical Effect of Color:

The wrong colors will dull the skin, eyes and hair, making you appear bland and tired. Your skin will show its texture more and your coloring will separate into blotchy patches if you wear colors that are not within your seasonal palette. Others' attention will be drawn to the thing that stands out most, whether it is your nose, chin, mouth, jaw, outfit or your make up ... but not to your eyes.

You were created with certain hair, skin and eye coloring that compliment each other. Maybe you don't like your coloring and have played with hair dye only to find you are now frustrated in trying to make your make up blend or your outfits look right.

Maybe you love soft, warm colors but always feel pasty and drawn when you wear them. Perhaps you often are asked if you are tired when you get plenty of sleep, and you never considered if it was the color of your blouse, for example, that made others ask that question.

Think of your body, your face, your hair, as a painter's canvas, any color you add to it (whether hair color, make up or clothing) should compliment the whole picture. You don't cover your canvas completely, so you want all the colors to compliment the undertones the Great Artist started you with.

If you have a soft, yellow-white canvas and you paint bright, bold cool colors on it, the colors will stand out from the canvas. The paint is what others will see. The uncovered canvas will be overpowered and unnoticed.

However, if you paint on other soft, yellow-toned colors, they will easily blend and compliment the canvas. Any untouched spot in the paint, where the canvas shows, will simply appear as part of the whole picture.

When others look at your image—your painting—you want the canvas (especially your eyes) to be what they see. It is not the outfit, your make up, or your hair coloring that you want noticed. It is you—your reflection of the glory of God—that you want to reveal to them.

When you are wearing your proper colors, you will receive compliments about *you*, how great *you* look. When you do a good job picking out outfits, but your choices are not your color, you may still hear compliments about the *outfit*, what a great dress you are wearing, but you may be lost in the picture.

You may feel good when someone says "that outfit is beautiful" or "that shirt looks great on you," but that doesn't mean that you are making the right color choices, it simply means that person likes that outfit or color, not that that outfit or color likes you. Often we choose our attire because of compliments we have received, but the compliments that we do best to listen to are the ones that speak about how we look, how others are seeing us—not our attire, our make up, or our shoes.

A great indication as to whether you are choosing proper colors for you is if you ever have trouble getting your makeup right or not. When you wear colors that compliment your skin tone, your make up will blend easily and your beauty will radiate. If you tend to wear colors that are not within your "seasonal palette," then you may always have difficulty with your make up. You may even have given up on wearing it at all.

If the compliments you hear are more about how "*you* look beautiful" or "*you* look great in that blouse," then you are probably closer to making choices that suit your Personal Image Identity.

I recommend that you consider having a color analyst help you discover your "seasonal palette." When you understand which colors compliment your features, it is wise to stay within that palette, especially when you are spending money on an outfit or make up. By paying for an analyst to teach you which colors you should purchase for yourself, you can save yourself a fortune on clothing and lipstick you liked on the rack, but look washed away in, or just won't go with anything else you have when you get it home.

One of the greatest benefits of knowing your color range and style is that when you bring a new piece of clothing into your closet, it should go well with what you already own.

Know the Emotional Effect of Color:

There is another important aspect to color. It helps to understand a little bit of the psychological effect color has on us. It can benefit you a lot to know that when you wear blue (pick the one within your season, of course) others will be drawn to you. Blue is universally accepted; we are not intimidated by it, but it shows power and authority in an inviting way. Blue is an excellent color to wear on a job interview or when meeting your potential in-laws …

Black, on the other hand, is simply powerful; it brings with it the respect of someone in authority. Yes, it is slimming, but if you are not a "Winter" it is not a good color for you, especially around your face. Black will draw the color out of anyone except a Winter and make her look lifeless. If you are a Winter, good for you, especially if you tend to stand before a group of people and teach or sell. You may have noticed that most pastors and businessmen wear dark suits. Black (or as close to black as you can be within your pallette) commands respect. It captures attention. People tend to believe what you have to say when you wear black.

Be careful, however, because black can be intimidating. Think about the kids who wear "Goth" clothing and makeup. Doesn't their presence say, "Keep away"? It is not just the chains and baggy clothes that make the statement. The fact that they are wearing all black, like a grieving widow, plays on our subconscious emotions. We are intimidated by them, and that is what they like, but the question is, is that what you like? Do you want others intimidated by your presence?

I know pastors and even some businessmen aren't as formal these days but have you ever noticed that those that are wearing suits are often also wearing a red tie? They understand a powerful tool. Black commands the respect they need to be effective, but their red tie stimulates the appetite. If we are at all interested in what the preacher or professional has to say, and he is wearing a dark suit and red tie, he commands our attention in a way that subconsciously makes us hungrier for what he is offering us.

It all can sound quite manipulative, I know, but I believe that if our subconscious minds play this game, so should our conscious ones.

If we have this knowledge of color, we would be fools to ignore it. It is one of those factors that is easy to forget, but at least try to remember it when you are shopping.

I do most of my own wardrobe shopping right before a speaking engagement. I am a summer, and black is simply not an option for me, especially if I am going to be under spotlights; I would disappear before the crowd! Also, my desire is not to take authority over those I am speaking to. I am a guest speaker, not their leader. So I want to wear a color that is powerful, but not intimidating. I usually pick blues or rosy browns.

Browns are very effective when trying to minister to someone who has a hard time opening up and sharing their heart with us. It is powerful but inviting. You may remember that most insurance men, when they come to your house to ask all the health questions, wear a brown suit. We tend to be less intimidated by brown, more free to be ourselves.

Know your Seasonal Palette of Color:

Basically, there are four seasonal palettes of color—Spring, Summer, Autumn, Winter. Your eye color, clarity and pattern of your eye structure, as well as the skin undertone (not its color), and the contrasts of these aspects with your hair (again, not necessarily the color) are all factors in deciding which season you are.

In order to discover your seasonal palette, you need to remove or hide all other influence of color, such as any makeup, hair, or clothing color you are already wearing as well as the lighting in the room. You want to know how each individual color influences your image.

This is very hard to do to yourself, and due to the emotional response your friends (and you) will have to color, it is not wise to simply trust others' opinion. Without doubt, there's enormous value in having a professional image consultant sort all this out for you by draping various fabrics over your neck and shoulder area to discover which colors make your skin tone, hair color and eyes become brighter and more alive.

Please be aware that not all makeup artists are certified color analysts. Do not be afraid to ask your analyst where she got her training. There are far too many sales people that are simply educated in color, but never tested or certified.

Your eye pattern and color and the chemical make up that causes your skin undertones and hair coloring does not change after age five. It does not mater how tan, wrinkled or gray you get; the season you are is the season you will remain for the rest of your days. You do not need to have this service repeated if it is done accurately. The money you spend on a consultation will be an investment for life.

Be sure to listen and take note of the things you are told by your analyst. Answering the questions below the best you can before your consultation, will help you get the most out of your investment:

What are your favorite colors?
What colors do you tend to choose for yourself?

- ❑ Bold, cool, crisp colors like black, white, reds
- ❑ Soft, cool, muted colors like steel gray, off white, pinks
- ❑ Bold, warm, bright colors like brown, yellows, peaches
- ❑ Soft, warm, muted colors like khaki, beige, oranges

How do you choose your hair, makeup and clothing colors?

- ❑ Based on your emotional response to the color
- ❑ Based on other people's comments
- ❑ Based on how my hair, skin and features respond to the color

What kind of skin tones do you have?

❑ Fair, porcelain, ivory or milky white
❑ Dark, deep, rich, tan
❑ Pink, rose beige, cool
❑ Peachy, golden beige, or coppery bronze, warm
❑ Freckled or ruddy (uneven complexion)
❑ Clear, healthy, radiant
❑ Dull, transparent, or pasty

What kind of hair coloring do you have?

❑ Light to medium brown, sandy or soft blonde, creamy gray, or natural highlights
❑ Medium to dark brown, black, silver gray, or a combination (salt and pepper)
❑ Auburn, red, golden brown, or true white
❑ Strawberry blond, honey or golden blonde, or creamy white

Do you prefer to color your hair?

❑ Yes, to cover the grey, with a solid color
❑ Yes, just for fun to add shine/color/pizzazz
❑ Yes, to blend the grey/ add texture, bring out highlights
❑ Yes, to add some color, depth and texture to some (lo-lights)
❑ Yes, to give some depth and texture with highlights
❑ No, I like to look natural

What color eyes do you have?

❑ Dark brown/black
❑ Light to medium brown
❑ Blue, gray blue, aqua, soft gray, teal
❑ Green, gray green, olive, yellow green
❑ Hazel, gold and green, gray and yellow

What kind of eye pattern do you have?

- ❑ Lacy or webbing, or cracked glass
- ❑ Spikes and spokes from pupil to iris edge
- ❑ Donut, star or sunlight shapes around pupil
- ❑ Flower petals around pupil
- ❑ Combination of any two or three above

What Your Color Analysis Knows:
Cool or blue undertone skin should wear cool, blue undertone colors.

Summer

If you have soft contrasts in your hair and skin, and have cool undertones, you are likely a Summer. Also, your hair may be "mousy" brown, light, medium or dark brown with auburn highlights, silvery gray, or light, medium or dark ash blonde (with a gray cast at the root).

The authors of "All Together You," Bette DeHaven and Ruth Milliron (interNet, 1995), whom I studied under to get my certification, describe the Summer palette as "soft, dusty, grayed and have a blue-based undertone. Now visualize a summer day. The sun shines more directly overhead causing the colors to become softer, especially if the humidity levels are high. A misty quality takes over the color of the sky and landscape. When you think of flowers like sweet peas, snap dragons, stock, etc., you can see the qualities of summer pinks, lavenders, white, etc."

If you are a Summer, and choose to color your hair, ask for highlights and/or lowlights, diversity in colors is beautiful on you and gives your hair depth. Stay away from warm undertones; cool, ash colors will look best.

When choosing your makeup, be sure your eyes are defined and have an appropriate cool color; without a little mascara or eyeliner your eyes can be washed away.

Winter

If you have strong, sharp contrasts in your hair and skin, and you have cool undertones, you are likely a winter. Also, your hair is most likely dark (black, dark, medium or light brown) or salt-n-pepper. Very rarely is a blonde a Winter, unless they are platinum or white blonde, or were as a child (sometimes tow-headed children grow up to become more honey-colored in adolescence, and more brown by the adult years, and can be mistaken for a spring).

DeHaven and Milliron write that "Winter hues are pure, clean, bold, and sharply contrasting. They are true primary or blue-based in undertone. Just visualize clean, new-fallen snow resting on wet, dark tree bark and pine needles, then contrast this against the crisp, deep blue sky of a winter day—then you have the essence of the winter color palette."

If you are a Winter, and choose to color your hair, be sure to color all the hair one shade. Stay away from warm undertones; you will do best with neutrals and cool tints.

When choosing your makeup, be sure your lips have an appropriate cool color, this will bring attention to your eyes.

What Your Color Analysis Knows:
Warm or yellow undertone skin should wear warm, yellow undertone colors.

Autumn
If you have soft contrasts in your hair and skin, and have warm undertones, you are likely a Autumn. Your skin may be very fair ivory or peachy; light to dark golden beige; golden black; or ruddy. Also, your hair may be strawberry or auburn red; honey or drab blonde with golden highlights; coppery red-brown; deep chestnut or golden brown; golden or dull gray; or maybe even charcoal black (although very rare).

DeHaven and Milliron describe your seasonal palette as, "warm, rich, earthy and mellow with a golden undertone in the yellow-base side of color. Picture New England trees that are breathtaking in all their golden, orange and red hues. As the sun sets, the landscape glows with warmth unequaled by anything I have ever seen."

If you are an Autumn and choose to color your hair, ask for highlights and/or lowlights; diversity in colors is beautiful on you and gives your hair depth. Stay away from cool undertones; warm, red colors are usually best for you.

When choosing your makeup, be sure your eyes are defined and have an appropriate warm color; without a little mascara or eyeliner your eyes can be washed away.

Spring

If you have strong contrasts in your hair and skin, and you have warm undertones, you are likely a Spring. Your skin may be ivory or milky white; peachy; ruddy and golden beige when tan. Also, your hair may be golden, honey or strawberry blonde; light, medium or deep red; golden brown (usually light); or dull, yellow gray.

Again, DeHaven and Milliron describe this palette in their book: "Spring hues are clean, clear and somewhat delicate in quality, but with a yellow-base or undertone. Freshness and clarity are the qualities of color this time of year. As you visualize springtime, all color, whether green, red, yellow or blue, seems to be warmed by the bright sunlight. It's especially easy to visualize the budding of new life in the springtime with its yellow-green quality."

If you are a Spring, and choose to color your hair, be sure to color all the hair one shade. Stay away from cool undertones. You will do best with neutrals and warm tints.

When choosing your makeup, be sure your lips have an appropriate warm color, as this will bring attention to your eyes.

My seasonal Palette is:
- ❑ Winter
- ❑ Summer
- ❑ Spring
- ❑ Autumn

Some of my best Colors:

_____

_____

CHAPTER SIXTEEN

CONFIDENT WITH YOUR PHYSICAL STATURE

Florists know how to care for each kind of flower in order for it to exude its greatest beauty. Movie stars and supermodels have image consultants who know which outfit is best on that girl's figure; that's why they always look so good.

So, what kind of beauty are you? Are you a delicate flower or an exotic one? I am sure you believe you are unique, and that you are imperfect. I hope you are discovering the rule of distraction and the power of modesty as well as the effects of color.

Now it is time to start applying all you know to your own body… but what kind of body do you have? Do you have a balanced, softly curved hourglass figure? Or is your balanced frame full-figured or straight? Do you have a figure that is broader at the shoulders or at the hips? What is your physical structure?

I encourage you to have a consultation by a professional. You can look in a mirror and decide what frame you have, but your vision will be distorted by your opinions of yourself and the memories of other peoples' opinions and responses to you. Your consultant will take a straight rod and show you whether you shoulders and hips are equal width or not; and whether your legs or torso are longer. She will consider whether your overall figure (your face, your waist, bust and derriere) is rounded or if you have straight lines and if you have an average, thick or delicate bone structure.

Most of all, she will give you the opinion of a non-biased professional on what not to wear so that you make choices from the many trends and styles that make "keeping up with the Joneses" so difficult in our fashion-driven society.

Let me tell you what I often tell my clients: You are your own worst critic. You tend to look at all your flaws, and compare them to others' strengths. But a professional won't judge you like that; she will assess you. Consider investing in an image consultation; it is a service most people will only need once, then for the rest of your life whether you gain weight, go grey or have many babies, her advice will help you in finding a wardrobe that suits you well. (Note: the only time you may want to have the service repeated is when you have forgotten everything you have been taught, or perhaps you have a major change in lifestyle, or weight or, for example, you now need to figure out how to dress like a business woman, or perhaps you have new curves that you never had to 'balance' before.)

As a professional myself I can't help but want to provide this valuable service for every one of my readers. Of course this is unrealistic, but through the years of doing group consultations I have worked hard on creating a system that walks you through the process of a self-analysis. You can find my pictorial survey on my website at www.CatrinaWelch.com or you can find it and a whole lot of practical advice to help you figure out which kind of outfits, hairstyle and makeup is best for you in my book Know Who You Are: Guidelines for your Personal Image Identity, which is available on my site as well. Because the details of finding your figure frame and how to balance any disproportions are all there, I am going to guide you through a very simple assessment here. I highly recommend either marking your answers in this book, or making a chart with a column for each Img.ID. Make a mark in each column for every character trait or preference that you have that relates to that Img.ID (if indicated.) At the end you will have one or two columns with more marks than the others; that will be your Img.ID.

In the example below, this Ingénue has many traits that could be another Img. ID, but her most dominant one indicates her true Img.ID.

	Classic	Natural	Dramatic	Ingénue	Romantic	Gamine
Frame	X	X	X	X		X
Height				X	X	X
Bone structure				X	X	X
Face	X	X	X	X	X	X
Eyes				X	X	X
Lips				X	X	X
Cheeks/chin				X	X	X
Nose				X	X	

No one fits in a box. Just as we each have unique fingerprints, so do we each have a blend of Img.IDs, but understanding which type of beauty we are is like knowing the culture your family comes from. If you are Italian, well that explains why conversations around your house are so animated. If you are Greek, well that might explain why Momma wants your wedding to be so big. Generalizations can be limiting, but analyzing your general beauty can be extremely helpful in understanding yourself and others, not to mention how much easier your shopping and daily preparation will be!

Your physical attributes indicate which culture or family you belong to. Your body frame is the foundation of all your image decisions. Basically, there are four body types: straight, curvy, full and sleek. Each body type is one of the five figure frames: A, H, 8, 0, and V (defined below); and each figure has its own strengths and challenges. You probably know your figure flaws already, but knowing your figure frame helps you to balance out any disproportions. There are lots of tips available (you can find some in my book of guidelines and on my site) to help you with this.

You cannot give yourself a fair makeover without knowing your physical stature. Your height is the greatest indicator. If you are tall, you are either a Dramatic or a Natural. If you are short, you are an Ingénue, a Romantic or a Gamine. If you are of average height, you could be any of the personalities.

To further determine which personality you are, it is best to assess your coloring (chapter 15). Depending on your seasonal palette of coloring, you may have to tone down or play up your Img.ID with a secondary clothing personality. For example, Gamines and Dramatics with a Summer or Autumn palette are often a combination of another clothing personality since the soft, muted colors make it difficult to be bold or create drama. Also, the softer-natured Img.IDs—Romantic,

Natural and Ingénue—with bold coloring may have a secondary personality to balance them out.

The third most important factor in determining your Img.ID is your facial features. This part, like the coloring, is hard to do in a book but I encourage you to do your best anyway. Ask a friend's opinion, or go to my website for pictures that will help. Whatever you do, though, please do not stress over this. Have fun with it.

Image Assessment: Physical Attributes

	Classic	Natural	Dramatic	Ingénue	Romantic	Gamine
Frame						
Height						
Bone structure						
Face						
Eyes						
Lips						
Cheeks/chin						
Nose						

Body Frame:

What is your figure frame?

- ❑ **Hourglass** *(balanced, softly curved) any of the Img.IDs*
- ❑ **V-frame** *(broader shoulders than hips) Classic, Natural, Romantic, Gamine*
- ❑ **H-frame** *(balanced, straight figure) Classic, Natural, Dramatic, Ingénue, Gamine*
- ❑ **8-frame** *(balanced, bust 10 inches greater than waist) Romantic*
- ❑ **O-frame** *(balanced, rounded tummy) Classic, Natural, Dramatic, Ingénue, Gamine*
- ❑ **A-frame** *(broader in hips than shoulders) Classic, Ingénue, Gamine*

If the above question is difficult for you, answer the question below to help you determine your figure frame. This question is not on your chart above, it's purpose is to help you figure out your frame, not necessarily your Img.ID. Every Img.ID could be any weight.

Where do you tend to gain weight first?
- ❑ Hips, lower body *(A- frame)*
- ❑ Bust, upper body *(V-frame)*
- ❑ Hips and Bust, always have waist-line even when overweight *(8-frame, hourglass)*
- ❑ Waist, midriff *(O-frame)*
- ❑ Weight gain has never been much of an issue *(H-frame, hourglass)*

What is your height? *This is the main determining feature of your Img.ID*
- ❑ **Tall:** 5'8" or more *(Natural, or Dramatic)*
- ❑ **Average:** 5'5"—5'7" *(Classic, Natural, Dramatic, Ingénue, Romantic or Gamine)*
- ❑ **Short:** 5'4" or less *(Ingénue, Romantic or Gamine)*

What is your bone structure? *Measure your wrist, if it is 6 inches your bone structure is average; if it is less than 5 ½ inches: you are petite-boned; if it is more than 6 ½ inches: you are broad-boned.*
- ❑ **Broad:** more than 6½" *(Natural, Dramatic)*
- ❑ **Average:** 5 ½"- 6 ½" *(Classic, Natural, Dramatic, Romantic, Ingénue, or Gamine)*
- ❑ **Petite:** less than 5 ½ " *(Romantic, Ingénue, Gamine)*

Facial Features:

Your facial structure is made up of not only the shape of your face, but also your facial silhouette and the way you hold your head over your body.

The ideal silhouette is balanced, with the head set squarely above the shoulders. When your nose or forehead are protruding, or if your head is set forward off your shoulders, you would do best to find a hairstyle that has fullness in the areas that will offset these features.

There are seven facial shapes, the ideal one being oval; if your face is any other shape, you will want your hair style to create illusions that will balance your features and give the appearance of an oval shape. Be sure than your facial shape is not repeated in your hairstyle. In other words, if you have a very round face, do not wear a rounded hairstyle such as a bob, instead follow some of the suggestion I give in my book of guidelines or on my website where you can also find some general rules for accessories, glasses and makeup as well as hair length and styles.

What is the shape of your face?

- ❑ **Oval** *(balanced, even, proportionate) could be any Img.ID*
- ❑ **Square** *(wide, angular jaw and forehead) Natural, Dramatic, Gamine*
- ❑ **Oblong** *(long, narrow, balanced) could be any Img.ID*
- ❑ **Diamond** *(narrow chin, brow; widest at cheeks) Natural, Dramatic, Gamine*
- ❑ **Heart** *(widest at forehead, narrow chin, often widow's peak hairline) Ingénue, Romantic*
- ❑ **Round** *(balanced, fullest at cheeks) Natural, Ingénue, Romantic, Gamine*
- ❑ **Pear** *(widest at jaw, narrow forehead) Natural, Dramatic, Ingénue, Romantic, Gamine*

What is the style of your eyes?

- ❑ Large, expressive, flirty *(Romantic, Gamine, Ingénue)*
- ❑ Average and proportionate *(Could be any Img.ID)*
- ❑ Friendly, or dramatic *(Natural, Dramatic)*

What is the type of your lips?

- ❑ Full *(Romantic, Ingénue)*
- ❑ Moderate, average *(Could be any Img.ID)*
- ❑ Thin *(Natural, Dramatic, Gamine)*

What are your cheeks and chin like?

- ❑ Somewhat flat cheekbone, average chin *(Classic)*
- ❑ Elongated or widely rounded *(Natural)*
- ❑ Prominent cheekbones and / or chin *(Dramatic)*
- ❑ Rounded cheeks and chin *(Romantic, Ingénue, Gamine)*

What style nose do you have?

- ❑ Average *(Could be any Img.ID)*
- ❑ Bluntly broad *(Natural)*
- ❑ Prominent *(Dramatic)*
- ❑ Straight *(Dramatic, Gamine)*
- ❑ Small *(Romantic, Ingénue)*
- ❑ Turned up *(Gamine)*

CHAPTER SEVENTEEN

CONFIDENT WITH YOUR CLOTHING PERSONALITY

While most women want to understand their image and enjoy analyzing their body frame and facial features, I find that many of us put up a guard when it comes to assessing our personality. No one wants to be critiqued, and limiting our individuality to one (or two) of six options can feel a bit like criticism, I know, but hear me out on this.

Let's liken our assessment to what a florist needs to do when she is caring for her various plants. With a quick glance she summarizes which type of flower she has and immediately she knows whether to water it daily, weekly or monthly. Some flowers she may give an ice cube to now and then because they need to receive water very slowly as the ice melts. There are some, like the Calla lily, that prefer shade, so she may put that flower in an area where she can protect it from the sun, while there are others she may put in full light to keep warm so that they may reach their full beauty.

Women are like that. Some of us need, or just want, extra care. Some prefer less fuss. Many are not sure what they want or need. What is right for one woman may be wrong for another, and too often we are confused as to which is which. Understanding our needs and our differences is what brings us Confident Beauty.

Some image consultants like Stacy London and Clinton Kelly from <u>What Not To Wear</u> may tell you what is right or wrong based on what's in vogue or according to your height or lifestyle, but I like to make it more personal in order to identify the true you. I often introduce myself as "an image consultant without the shopping obsession; my message is not so much '*what not to wear*' as it is '*Know Who You Are*' which is the title of my book of guidelines for your Personal Image Identity."

As much as I believe that God does not want us to judge each other by our outward appearance, I also believe that the outward character often indicates what is on the inside, and that is what really matters.

The challenge I run into when assessing women is when their preferences do not line up with their physical stature. This is very common for girls who were raised by a woman with a different Img.ID. We naturally form our opinions on what feminine beauty should be through personal experience. Influential women in our lives either help us decide if we want to be like them, or not. Perhaps your mom was a Classic who taught you to keep a proper and professional wardrobe but you just wanted to be carefree and feminine with your look. Your choice is to comply with her style and feel confined and constricted, or to choose your own manner of expressing your individuality. A lot of times your unique style includes many aspects of the feminine influences in your life mixed in with what you like. Other times you may need to decide to change things that worked for her, but do not work well for you.

Typically, each clothing personality has a particular type of fashion that is most important to them and something that they need to be careful not to get out of balance in order to achieve their personal "look."

Classic:
- Priority: to be well put together and ladylike
- Look: timeless, but fashionable
- Caution: can become boring, predictable, too conservative

Natural:
- Priority: comfort!
- Look: sporty, casual or "country"
- Caution: can become masculine, outdated, too plain or dumpy

Dramatic
- Priority: to have the latest look; accessorizing
- Look: high fashion, trendy, modern
- Caution: can be cheap, tacky or lacking in class

Ingénue
- Priority: to be dainty or "girly"
- Look: very feminine, but innocent vs. sexy
- Caution: can be too reserved and shy; also can become very outdated

Romantic
- Priority: others! Or to hide self
- Look: curvy, soft and feminine
- Caution: can tend to look cheap or provocative if not careful

Gamine
- Priority: comfort, control
- Look: petite, sporty, bouncy, fun
- Caution: can become masculine, outdated, too plain or dumpy

In the last chapter we assessed which personality your physique best represents. Now we are going to assess the final indicator as to which one (or combination of two) you are. If you find that you are a combination of personalities, the dominant personality is determined by your physical stature (from last chapter). Your secondary personality is determined by your personal preferences (see survey below). When you put all this together with your coloring, your lifestyle, and your outside influences, you have your Personal Image Identity, your Img.ID.

So let's get to know you. If you find answering the questions to be difficult (which is not uncommon—especially for women who have never had the freedom to make choices for their own lives), I encourage you to seek God's help on the matter. Ask Him to show you how He sees you; ask Him to stir up in you the desires that He placed deep in your heart. Allow Him to show you what has happened in your life that has made you indifferent or indecisive. Read His Word, and listen for Him to speak to you regarding your heart.

Your opinions do have value. You are allowed to make choices in your life. You can be who God made you to be. You do not need to be the woman that men, media and your mom have persuaded you to be. You are free to be you!

Remember to continue adding marks to the columns on your chart of clothing personalities. Here is another chart to help you:

Image Assessment: Personal Preferences

	Classic	Natural	Dramatic	Ingénue	Romantic	Gamine
Lifestyle/ career						
Attire/ wardrobe						
Makeup						
Social events						
Hosting parties						

What kind of lifestyle/career do you live, or desire to live?

❑ Administration/management/accounting. I like to work with numbers and organize people and events. I am task-oriented. *(Classic)*

❑ Homemaker/anything to do with nature or sports. I like a simple, carefree kind of life. *(Natural)*

❑ Professional/ business owner/ artist. I want to be my own boss; I'm a free spirit. *(Dramatic)*

❑ Designer/ Decorator. I love to be creative. *(Ingénue)*

❑ Advertising/recruiting/service. I love to help people. I tend to promote things I believe in. *(Romantic)*

❑ Sales/marketing/public relations/nursing/law/cheerleading. I am bold. I could sell anything I believe in. I don't have a problem with correcting people. *(Gamine)*

What do you feel is most important when choosing your attire?

❑ That it is well put together, complete *(Classic)*

❑ That it is comfortable, casual *(Natural)*

❑ That it is stylish, up to date and accessorized *(Dramatic)*

❑ I don't know. That it is feminine or "girly" *(Ingénue)*

❑ That it's sexy… or that it hides my body… or simply that it fits! *(Romantic)*

❑ That I like it. It's fun, yet comfortable and colorful *(Gamine)*

How do you feel about makeup?

❑ It's a "necessary evil," not something to talk about, just wear it. *(Classic)*

❑ It's uncomfortable / I think it's silly, vain or unnecessary. *(Natural)*

❑ Love it, and enjoy being creative with it. *(Dramatic)*

❑ I don't feel strongly either way, but it shouldn't be obvious. (Ingénue)

❑ It makes me feel prettier, so I do it. *(Romantic)*

❑ I don't want to have to wear it, but I will when I want to dress up. *(Gamine)*

How do you feel about social events?

❑ I want them organized and structured. *(Classic)*

❑ I could take them or leave them- if it is a fancy event I may stress a bit because I have to dress up. *(Natural)*

❑ I enjoy parties- the fancier the better. I love a reason to dress up. *(Dramatic)*

❑ I prefer simple, intimate parties, but cheerfully attend any for the other people's sake. *(Ingénue)*

❑ I prefer small parties and only with people I know and love. *(Romantic)*

❑ I don't mind a party at all; in fact I am often told I'm the life of the party; although if it's not "my kind of people/purpose" I'd rather be doing the dishes. *(Gamine)*

How would you entertain if you were the hostess in charge?

❑ I want plenty of time to plan. I give careful attention to all the details. I would prepare a "tried and true" recipe. *(Classic)*

❑ I don't get worked up over parties unless I'm expected to make it all fancy. I prefer simple, casual, self-serve parties served on paper goods. I prepare whatever is on hand. *(Natural)*

❑ I prefer to have plenty of notice so that I can take care of every detail with excellence; but if it's a spontaneous party I need to throw, I will still do as many extras as I can find time for—like gourmet food and striking décor. *(Dramatic)*

❑ If I need to host a party, I would kindly do whatever I need to, and not ask for any help. I would prepare my guest of honor's favorite food and would be very creative in order to make my guests feel very special. *(Ingénue)*

❑ I will make it an elegant event. My home will have candlelight, music, potpourri, lace and fine food. I will serve my guests well and be sure every need is met. It is hard for me to sit down and enjoy the party. *(Romantic)*

❑ If I need to host the event, I might make reservations at a restaurant, or have it catered. My parties are not a lot of work but they are a lot of fun! *(Gamine)*

Answer Key

Looking at each of your charts, which clothing personality did you mark the most?

Did the two charts have the same column marked more than the others? If not, you may have a secondary clothing personality; be sure to read the chapter on both of the personalities that you marked most. In the final chapter I will go over combination personalities and how to blend the guidelines together in order to best represent the true you.

If your answers were all over the place, and you are not sure which personality is strongest, do not worry. You may be an Ingénue, or a Classic; be sure to read those chapters to see if it suits you or not. Also, no matter what your chart looks like, be sure to read the chapter on each clothing personality if you want to understand the other women in your life better!

❑ **Classic—Refined Beauty** Average height and features. Professional. Calm, poised, warm, gracious, refined, polished, elegant. Cultured, meticulous; usually well-educated.

❑ **Natural—Casual Beauty** Average to tall. Broad features. Casual, unpretentious. Conservative, practical, reliable, dependable, responsible loyal; usually well-loved.

❑ **Dramatic—Exotic Beauty** (sophisticated or artsy and eccentric) Average to tall. Exotic features. Unique, imaginative, independent, sophisticated, demanding, stylish; usually well-known.

❑ **Ingénue—Delicate Beauty** Average to short. Youthful features. Sweet, gentle, soft, graceful, youthful, modest, shy, considerate, supportive; usually well-appreciated.

❑ **Romantic—Feminine Beauty** Average to short. Soft features. Feminine, charming, sensitive, sympathetic, accommodating. Sensual, alluring, glamorous, flirtatious. Usually found desirable by others.

❑ **Gamine—Bold Beauty** Average to short. Animated features. Fun, energetic, enthusiastic. Bold, bouncy, snappy, spunky charmer; usually well-respected.

PART THREE

THE PRACTICAL SIDE OF CONFIDENT BEAUTY:
The Makeover

Because Confidence is Knowing Who You Are

CHAPTER EIGHTEEN

CONFIDENT CLASSIC

The Refined Beauty

Classic

Body type:

- Average height (5'4" to 5'7") and build.
- Moderately sized hands, wrists, feet.
- Usually a figure A or H in body frame.
- Balanced in structure (not delicate or stalky).
- Silhouette may be softly straight.
- Mature in appearance and personality.

Facial features:

- Symmetrical, not long, wide or angular.
- Average to attractive, balanced features.

Hair:

- Naturally smooth, evenly textured hair.
- May be wavy or straight.

Character: *The Classic woman is the epitome of elegance, especially if she is a Summer or Spring; although she can be any season.*

If I were to choose a woman from the Bible who best represents a Classic, I would choose the Virgin Mary. You find her story throughout the gospels of Matthew and Luke. As a young lady, Mary was levelheaded and poised. She was a proper girl who was committed to following the social standards of her day. When an angel appeared to her and told her she would be pregnant she remained poised but she needed to know how that would happen since she was a virgin.

Now in the sixth month the angel Gabriel was sent by God to a city of Galilee named Nazareth, to a virgin betrothed to a man whose name was Joseph, of the house of David. The virgin's name was Mary. And having come in, the angel said to her, "Rejoice, highly favored one, the Lord is with you; blessed are you among women!"

But when she saw him, she was troubled at his saying, and considered what manner of greeting this was. Then the angel said to her, "Do not be afraid, Mary, for you have found favor with

God. And behold, you will conceive in your womb and bring forth a Son, and shall call His name Jesus. He will be great, and will be called the Son of the Highest; and the Lord God will give Him the throne of His father David. And He will reign over the house of Jacob forever, and of His kingdom there will be no end."

Then Mary said to the angel, "How can this be, since I do not know a man?" And the angel answered and said to her, "The Holy Spirit will come upon you, and the power of the Highest will overshadow you; therefore, also, that Holy One who is to be born will be called the Son of God. Now indeed, Elizabeth your relative has also conceived a son in her old age; and this is now the sixth month for her who was called barren. For with God nothing will be impossible."

Then Mary said, "Behold the maidservant of the Lord! Let it be to me according to your word." And the angel departed from her. **Luke 1:26-38**

Was she being asked to break the rules and sleep with a man before marriage? My presumption is that if that had been the case she would have refused the offer and told the angel to go away. But it wasn't the case, so instead she took on the incomprehensible responsibility of carrying the Christ Child, and she did it with tremendous faith and confidence. In fact, all throughout her life as the mother of Jesus, the Bible says she pondered in her heart the things she heard and saw as her baby's Deity was revealed.

Classics are thinkers and planners. They watch what is going on around them, they study, they gain wisdom and they act on their knowledge without concern for their reputation. They do what is right even if others do not understand them. In fact, once they are convinced of something it is very hard to get them to change their mind.

Classics live a balanced life, they tend to eat right and exercise, they work hard and take the vacation time they earn. The Classic is not only organized and orderly, but she needs to be; in fact, chaos will quite often bring out the worst in her. When things get out of control she may get stressed, but rarely does she get caught up in the moment. She may be emotional by nature, but she is controlled and rational in mannerism.

I use the rose to represent the Classic because she is a refined beauty. She is dignified and sophisticated and stable in all her ways. She is graceful and conservative and a pleasure to look at. She has a balanced figure and proportionate features and tends to have her professional look all together, with everything coordinated and accessorized, (though it may be outdated).

This woman is hard to get close to. Like the rose, she has a guard about her. In her younger years she is tight and withdrawn and a bit protective of her heart and habits. When she is upset she may speak with sharp words, but she doesn't have to say much. People respect her. As she matures she opens up and those willing to risk knowing her can easily remove her thorns. Her wisdom and skills are often a sweet aroma to those who need her.

We all need a Classic in our lives; they make great mentors. Unfortunately, many Classics are left to pursue their great ambitions alone because those that don't understand her passion to make things better may consider her critical, or stuck in her ways, but those that know her will agree that her stability brings security and her wisdom and administrative skills are valuable.

Like the rose, this woman's elegant beauty is best enjoyed when it is complimenting other types of beauty. A single rose in a vase is lovely but a rose properly placed in a bouquet, or surrounded by baby's breath is captivating and inviting. Most women guard their hearts by determining to not need others. The Classic, especially, needs to fight the tendency to stand alone. Others need what she has to offer, and she needs others to accentuate what she has to offer.

One example of this is in home decorating. If you were to enter a Classic's home you most likely will find a beautiful, high quality house and furnishings that are missing the finishing touches of the decorative details. This is typical of most areas of the Classic's life; they have excellent, detailed dreams and ambitions but often their efforts are left incomplete.

Perhaps that's why God planned Elizabeth's pregnancy with John the Baptist so close to Mary's pregnancy. Classic women who realize that they need the counsel and expertise of other women are powerfully productive. I know raising children can seem like more of a distraction from productivity than anything powerful, but think of how carefully God chose the mother of His Child. This pregnancy changed Mary's life and she chose to live out the honor set before her. To her credit, she did not choose to do it alone. Mary spent three months studying under the wisdom of her cousin who was in the last trimester of her own miracle.

Now Mary arose in those days and went into the hill country with haste, to a city of Judah, and entered the house of Zacharias and greeted Elizabeth. And it happened, when Elizabeth heard the greeting of Mary, that the babe leaped in her womb; and Elizabeth was filled with the Holy Spirit. Then she spoke out with a loud voice and said, "Blessed are you among women, and blessed is the fruit of your womb! But why is this granted to me, that the mother of my Lord should come to me? For indeed, as soon as the voice of your greeting sounded in my ears, the babe leaped in my womb for joy. Blessed is she who believed, for there will be a fulfillment of those things which were told her from the Lord."
Luke 1: 39-45

Elizabeth was a lot older than Mary. While it's wise to seek counsel from those who have gone before us, I imagine Mary didn't have many other options. Classics are usually quite serious, task-oriented people. Their friends may leave them out of fun events for fear they may make it too complicated. Most of their social circles are professional in nature. I doubt there were many networking events in Mary's day, so I assume she lived a very simple and private life. That is, until the news got out …

When challenges come into our lives all privacy flees. People talk. Sometimes it's because they care, other times it's because it's fun to share the news—even if it's none of their business. It stinks to be the topic of gossip. Imagine the rejection Mary had to deal with because of the "honor" bestowed on her. I was pregnant and alone in a culture that accepts unwed moms; Mary's culture stoned adulterers.

Not everyone understands the Classic. Especially people who don't want to follow rules; they can't even fathom anyone liking rules, never mind the Classic's passion to keep things proper. Her professional nature makes them feel inadequate. When Mary apparently "messed up," surely there was a lot of gossip and backbiting going on. She was wise to get away for a little while and spend some time with another woman of God who could affirm her and encourage her.

Mary returned to her people and took responsibility for her life. She may have felt their judgment, but she did not let them stop her from doing what she knew she was called to do. The rest of her life emitted Confident Beauty, like an open rose's fragrant offering to those around her.

If you are a Classic, you are elegant, and you are organized. You take responsibility seriously, yet you tend to keep a low profile, even if you are a highly respected woman of prestige. Your image should elegantly reflect that prestige and modesty.

Your Motto: Proper elegance

Suggestions:
- Relax a little with the formalities in life.
- Start with your image.

Remember: *"First impressions are lasting impressions." When you expect high standards of yourself, others assume that you expect the same of them, and they may feel intimidated by that.*
- Don't compromise who you are.
- Be sure to give others the freedom to be who they are, too.

Your wardrobe:
- Soft, modest, all-together image.
- Traditional looks, especially professional suits.
- Avoid any extremes: textures, lines, colors.
- Ensemble dresser.
- Does not need to be extravagant, but must have coordinating accessories.
- Coordinate everything from head to toe, including belts, bags and shoes.

Caution:
By definition, "Classic" does not change much over the years, and because of this the Classic may not be concerned about her wardrobe being up to date; her only concern is that it is complete. Typically, she does not shop often.
- Be careful not to let your wardrobe get outdated, or you will come across as matronly.
- Be aware of the level of formality in your casual outfits; save the fancy accessories for fancy events.

Shopping Tips: *You are a woman of balance, so should your image be.*
- Give yourself permission to shop, or you can become boring or predictable with your attire.
- Do not choose styles that are too conservative, or you may become lost in the plainness.
- Choose fashion trends (not fads) to stay current and fashionable.
- Choose stores that are fashionable, defined and contemporary. Only shop there.
- Purchase quality clothing, since you will hold onto your outfits for years.
- Focus on a base color scheme, especially if money is limited.
- Always invest in solid colors first, and coordinate your accessories in that color.
- Complete one outfit at a time.

Your fabrics:

Nothing about you is extreme; your lines, accents and fabrics should not be either. That means not too rough, heavy, stiff, clingy or sheer.
- Look for richness and quality in moderate weights.
- Be careful that your fabrics are not too drapey or too tailored.
- Avoid crisp or bouffant lines; you will do best with lines that are soft or softly flared.
- Choose refined textures such as silk, soft woolens and cottons, and smooth knits.
- Low luster and matte finishes are best for you.
- Solid colors should be your first choice.
- When choosing a print, find evenly balanced patterns that are easy on the eye.

Formal Attire:
- Chiffons and elegantly beaded outfits.
- Monochromatic, but nothing too boring. Choose your best colors.

Makeup:
- Should be polished, flawless
- Simple, natural and neutral in colors
- Nothing dramatic

Accessories:

You wear accessories well. Be sure they are:
- Refined, elegant, and timelessly fashionable.
- Avoid angles and straight lines; choose smooth geometric or circular accessories.
- Costume jewelry is fine as long as it's of good quality.
- Avoid dainty dangles or anything "funky."
- When it comes to shoes, choose classic pumps or sling backs.
- You look great in scarves, especially silk or challis ones.

Hairstyle:
- You should wear a smooth, controlled style such as a bob or bun.
- Ideally, your hair should be moderate in length, or somewhat short.
- It is important that you maintain your haircuts and color, and keep your hairstyle well-groomed.

Manicure:
- Should be smooth and classy.
- Polished, but not necessarily with color.
- Stay within your seasonal palette of colors.
- Edges are best rounded, smooth, even.

CHAPTER NINETEEN

CONFIDENT NATURAL

The Casual Beauty

Natural

Body type:

- Average to tall in height (usually at least 5'7").
- Strong and sturdy, muscular.
- Hips may be curvy with a nice waistline or straight with a thick waist.
- Bone structure is softly angular.
- Shoulders may be broad to average in width.
- Strong hands (usually size 6" wrist or more).

Facial features:

- Broad (round or square) or long (oblong).
- Features may be uneven or asymmetrical with blunt edges (especially on a broad face).
- Nose may be broad and flat.

Hair:

- May be fine, coarse or average.
- May be curly or straight.

Character: *The Natural woman is the epitome of casual beauty; she is a sporty, outdoors kind of gal who makes others comfortable around her, because she is comfortable with herself.*

Like a Gerbera Daisy, this style of beauty is simple and playful. The Natural's bright cheer brings life to any occasion, making a formal affair even more fun and a casual event more inviting. Like the flower that only requires basic care and sunlight, the Natural's carefree nature should not be overdone with too much attention to details. She is strong and sturdy and able to endure most environments as long as she is not overwatered or placed where there is no sun. The one area of concern this beauty does need to pay attention to is in maintaining her beauty. The flower needs to have old blossoms removed or they will suck the life out of the plant's ability to bloom more. The Natural needs to do the same with her wardrobe. She has her favorite items of clothing and may continue to wear them even after they are worn out or stained, which will drain the life out of her beauty.

If I were to choose a woman from the Bible who best represents the Natural Img.ID, I would choose Abigail. You find the story of this strong and confident woman in 1 Samuel 25. She was the wife of Nabal, a rich and abusive man who showed no compassion. When David and his men asked Nabal for food after they had been protecting his shepherds and flocks, he refused to give them anything.

———————— ✳ ✻ ✳ ————————

Now there was a man in Maon whose business was in Carmel, and the man was very rich. He had three thousand sheep and a thousand goats. And he was shearing his sheep in Carmel. The name of the man was Nabal, and the name of his wife Abigail. And she was a woman of good understanding and beautiful appearance; but the man was harsh and evil in his doings. He was of the house of Caleb.

When David heard in the wilderness that Nabal was shearing his sheep, David sent ten young men; and David said to the young men, "Go up to Carmel, go to Nabal, and greet him in my name. And thus you shall say to him who lives in prosperity: 'Peace be to you, peace to your house, and peace to all that you have! Now I have heard that you have shearers. Your shepherds were with us, and we did not hurt them, nor was there anything missing from them all the while they were in Carmel...

Now one of the young men told Abigail, Nabal's wife, saying, "Look, David sent messengers from the wilderness to greet our master; and he reviled them. But the men were very good to us, and we were not hurt, nor did we miss anything as long as we accompanied them, when we were in the fields. They were a wall to us both by night and day, all the time we were with them keeping the sheep. Now therefore, know and consider what you will do, for harm is determined against our master and against all his household. For he is such a scoundrel that one cannot speak to him."

Then Abigail made haste and took two hundred loaves of bread, two skins of wine, five sheep already dressed, five seahs of roasted grain, one hundred clusters of raisins, and two hundred cakes of figs, and loaded them on donkeys. And she said to her servants, "Go on before me; see, I am coming after you." But she did not tell her husband Nabal.

So it was, as she rode on the donkey, that she went down under cover of the hill; and there were David and his men, coming down toward her, and she met them. Now David had said, "Surely in vain I have protected all that this fellow has in the wilderness, so that nothing was missed of all that belongs to him. And he has repaid me evil for good. May God do so, and more also, to the enemies of David, if I leave one male of all who belong to him by morning light." **1 Samuel 25:2-7, 14-22**

Abigail recognized that her husband was wrong and that his rude nature had put her whole family's life at stake, so she got on her donkey and pursued David to make things right.

Natural beauties are like that; they can just jump on a donkey and ride into the wind looking all cute with their hair a mess. They aren't as concerned for themselves as they are others. More than likely, Abigail had put up with abuse for years, but now that someone else was in danger, she was going to do something about it.

Naturals don't really care about what other people think; they care about helping people. They are dependable and loyal women who are not afraid of work. They will do whatever it takes to encourage those they love. Abigail may not have loved David (yet…), but she knew he was anointed to be king and that his humble request for food was not unreasonable. His men were starving and her family was having a feast. By nature a Natural is faithful and supportive; when she hears of the needs of others, she wants to meet them. It must have killed Abigail inside to learn that her husband was rebuffing someone in need… especially knowing that someone was going to be her king!

Verse 18 says that this brave woman quickly made two hundred loaves of bread, added two skins of wine, five sheep already dressed, five "seahs" of roasted grain, one hundred clusters of raisins, and two hundred cakes of figs, and then loaded the food on donkeys. That sounds like a Natural to me: They do what they need to do, and don't worry if it's looking or smelling fine. They are very practical people. They work quickly and productively because they don't get hung up on the time-consuming details that aren't important to them.

It may have been her culture and time, but I am assuming Abigail's preference was a simple, informal and unstructured life. If this Img.ID is going to host a party she would actually prefer it not be planned so she can excuse that it is thrown in a basket and loaded onto a donkey. If she is at a party, she would rather not be, unless it's a backyard BBQ or buffet-style at a good friend's home. I bet Abigail loved the chance to get away from that feast to do something more important, like saving her family.

Natural women usually have good people skills. I believe Abigail must have qualified there, too. She was living with an abusive man, but his temperament did not defeat her. Some of us are paralyzed by a man's anger. Abigail was not. She knew how to handle her husband's foolishness, and she did it without dishonoring him. She sent others ahead of her, and went the secret pathway toward David in order to protect him from knowing what she was doing until the right time to tell him.

Nabal was not worthy of honor, but she did show him respect. David did earn honor, and Abigail quickly demonstrated that when she reached him. She fell on her face and bowed down before his feet and apologized for her husband's rude behavior.

Very often abused women take responsibility for the wrongdoing of others, and try to cover up their mistakes, especially those of their abuser. Abigail did that, but she did so with wisdom and boundaries. She was determined to correct Nabal's foolishness, she was determined to protect her household, and she was also determined to keep David from making a big mistake himself. Codependency is something women can tend to be prone to, but it is not always a bad trait. I think God is pleased with us when we invest so much into others, as long as we keep a clear head and our focus is on His will not our own.

Abigail had healthy codependency.

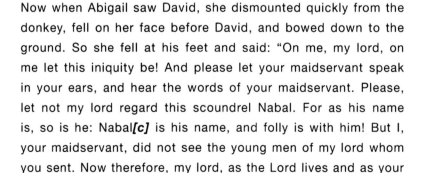

Now when Abigail saw David, she dismounted quickly from the donkey, fell on her face before David, and bowed down to the ground. So she fell at his feet and said: "On me, my lord, on me let this iniquity be! And please let your maidservant speak in your ears, and hear the words of your maidservant. Please, let not my lord regard this scoundrel Nabal. For as his name is, so is he: Nabal[c] is his name, and folly is with him! But I, your maidservant, did not see the young men of my lord whom you sent. Now therefore, my lord, as the Lord lives and as your soul lives, since the Lord has held you back from coming to bloodshed and from avenging yourself with your own hand, now then, let your enemies and those who seek harm for my lord be as Nabal. And now this present which your maidservant has brought to my lord, let it be given to the young men who follow my lord. Please forgive the trespass of your maidservant. For the Lord will certainly make for my lord an enduring house, because my lord fights the battles of the Lord, and evil is not found in you throughout your days. Yet a man has risen to pursue you and seek your life, but the life of my lord shall be bound in the bundle of the living with the Lord your God; and the lives of your enemies He shall sling out, as from the pocket of a sling. And it shall come to pass, when the Lord has done for my lord according to all the good that He has spoken concerning you, and has appointed you ruler over Israel, that this will be no grief to you, nor offense of heart to my lord, either that you have shed blood without cause, or that my lord has avenged himself. But when the Lord has dealt well with my lord, then remember your maidservant." **1 Samuel 25:23-31**

She successfully brought the king's perspective back to proper priorities and saved her family by simply reminding him that God fights his battles and that he should keep himself from shedding innocent blood. Her motive wasn't all about covering up what her husband did wrong; we know that because she did not keep what she did a secret. When she got back to Nabal he was drunk, so she waited until the next morning to tell him what happened. If her desire was to manipulate things for her own good, she wouldn't have told him at all.

It seems that most Naturals have a lot of faith. They are simple, realistic people, but they tend to lean toward optimism no matter how bad life can be. Abigail encouraged the king to stay his course; she didn't panic and plead with him for favor and forgiveness. She remained calm, cool and collected and reasoned with two very upset men, each according to their nature and circumstances. In the end, God did for Abigail the very thing she reminded David He would do for him: He fought her battle, too.

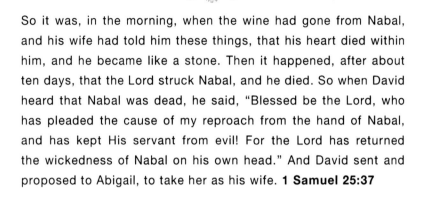

So it was, in the morning, when the wine had gone from Nabal, and his wife had told him these things, that his heart died within him, and he became like a stone. Then it happened, after about ten days, that the Lord struck Nabal, and he died. So when David heard that Nabal was dead, he said, "Blessed be the Lord, who has pleaded the cause of my reproach from the hand of Nabal, and has kept His servant from evil! For the Lord has returned the wickedness of Nabal on his own head." And David sent and proposed to Abigail, to take her as his wife. **1 Samuel 25:37**

People are drawn to the Natural woman because of her casual approach to life; she makes them comfortable around her. She has a carefree attitude that is seldom offended; but because of this, she can get stuck in a stagnant place of living her life for others instead of following her calling.

The Natural woman does well in outdoor, sporty or people-oriented careers, especially ones requiring casual attire or a uniform, because she is usually inclined to wear comfortable, sporty clothes and she doesn't care much about fashion. It can be hard for her to find her true desires about her image for fear of appearing vain or self-absorbed, and it's often difficult for her to understand the Beauty Battle that others struggle with. Others may misunderstand her laid-back nature to be laziness, especially if she begins to neglect herself (as a Natural can do when she gets discouraged) but they seldom doubt her loyalty or faithfulness.

Natural beauties that find balance are strong and steady women who are relatable and inspiring. This world needs women like them.

If you are a Natural, you are simple, reasonable and sporty. Your image should reflect who you are.

Your Motto: Keep it simple. Less is more. *(Less detail is more appealing on you.)*

Suggestions: *You need to know that you deserve to look lovel,y too! Because your beauty is simple does not mean it is less valuable; in fact, your sheer, simple beauty will encourage those around you far more than most clothing personalities. Your very presence calls others to a higher (yet peaceful) level of femininity.*

- Realize that dressing up not only displays self-respect, it shows respect to the host or the occasion you are attending.
- Enjoy the beauty God gave you to share with those around you. Do not let the enemy steal your joy, making you feel as if you are vain.

Your Wardrobe: *Your look is freshly appealing; your garments should have no fuss and minimal detail. Simple, comfortable things are what look great on you anyway!*
- Your look is unstructured; if it is tailored at all, it is only simple and soft tailoring that works for you.
- Jeans, T-shirts and sweat suits are allowed; in fact, these are a great option on you!

Caution: *Looking good is not the Natural's priority, but being comfortable is a priority that can throw her image out of balance; and that can destroy her feminine beauty, making her unapproachable and unrelatable.*
- Don't repeat your favorite outfits too often.
- Avoid masculine clothing, no matter how comfortable.
- Be careful not to "let yourself go."

You want to be comfortable, there is nothing wrong with that; wear those sporty outfits and jeans… Just be sure:
- They have some style (find a designer sweat suit!).
- They are clean, neat, and still in good repair.

Remember, you, too are the daughter of a King, and a Princess should be treated as such.

Shopping tips: *Since you don't like to shop, stay away from discount stores, because you will become frustrated when they don't have your look, or when you find something that does work for you and it doesn't last, since you will wear it every chance you get!*
- Choose mix-and-match separates.
- Choose many textures and colors; these look youthful and fashionable on you.

Only purchase clothing within your seasonal palette of colors; that way when you bring home a new garment it will mix and match with the ones you already have.

Your Fabrics: *Pay attention to your fabrics; they are the main factor in your wardrobe. Always wear some texture; some great choices are:*

- Woven or knitted garments that are soft, rough or nubby.
- Crinkled and wrinkled looks are flattering on you.
- Raw silks, tweeds, flannels, linens, cottons and denims.

Formal Attire: *Formal to you is not the same as it is to the other clothing personalities. When you dress within your clothing personality, even in your most formal attire, you are not intimidating, but inviting to others. Glamour and possessions are not your concern in life, but remember it is not selfish or wrong to look glamorous at times.*

- Your look is simple elegance.
- Great choices: Sheath, strapless gown or a simple sarong.
- Look for crepes, microfibers and velvets.
- Chanel beading is a great glamorous look on you.

Makeup:

- Natural, minimal.
  ◊ Foundation (even just powder).
  ◊ Lip gloss (Winter, Spring) or Mascara (Summer, Autumn).
- Do not overdo it, even on formal occasions.

Accessories: *Typically, most Naturals wear the same jewelry every day. That is OK! Keep it minimal; too many details tend to look awkward on you anyway.*

- Find a good quality belt, handbag and shoes, and stick with them.
- Choose simple chains and stud earrings.
- If you like a bit of flare, choose chunky or funky, earthen or Indian jewels.
- Do not choose pearls.

Hairstyle: *Wash-and-wear is officially acceptable for you! Flat iron may be OK, but if your hair looks "set" in anyway (curling iron, firm blow dry), you will look matronly. Do not spend too much time on your hair.*

- Tousled, loose, windblown looks do well on you.
- Avoid smooth, sleek looks of all kinds (unless you are partly Classic).

Manicures:

- Clean, smooth, rounded edges.
- Minimal length.
- French manicure, clear or no polish.

CHAPTER TWENTY

CONFIDENT DRAMATIC

The Exotic Beauty

Dramatic

It is important to note that there are many Dramatic "wannabes." Adding drama to any personality livens it up and is more fun, and really, "girls just wanna have fun!" But only a true Dramatic can carry off extremes. In fact, this is really the only woman who can wear heavy makeup or much jewelry and not come across as cheap.

You are a true Dramatic if your body is the frame and cut of a Dramatic. If your personal preferences alone are the Dramatic influence, then this could be your secondary personality.

There are two types:

Sophisticated Dramatic: Excellence, quality, detailed
Artsy or Trendy Dramatic: Extreme, exotic, eccentric

Body type:

- Usually tall and slender, but may be average height and slender, or tall and heavy.
- Typically exotic and straight figure.
- Sleek but sturdy build.
- Long, slender hands and feet (size 9 or more shoe).
- Square, sharp or angular neck and shoulder lines.

Facial features:

- Sharply angular or defined features.
- Unusually exotic in appearance.
- May have a prominent nose, high chiseled cheekbones or angular jaw line.
- When made up, eyes may be striking.

Hair:

- Usually straight, or extreme curls.
- May be fine, frizzy or coarse.

Character: *The Dramatic is a fast-paced, hardworking woman who is not afraid to take risks. She has a daring nature that is seemingly uninhibited by the influences around her but the truth is she often has a very sensitive spirit.*

She is like an exotic flower, of which, of course, there are many kinds. I use the Protea to represent the Artsy Dramatic and the Bird of Paradise for the Sophisticated Dramatic. The Dramatic with a flare for art can carry off a costume-like image and come across as fun- like a Protea with its very unusual kind of beauty. The Dramatic who is more sophisticated also stands out with her unique style, but she may be more often included in social circles. Add an exotic flower to any bouquet and it will make a statement at your party; add a lot of them and it may be too much, unless it is a formal event or held in an exquisite hotel. These women sometimes come across as "too much" when they are together. Their animated character to their unique beauty seems to draw the assumption that they want all the attention, but like the flowers they actually do better in indirect sunlight and away from where they can be touched. It may take time for this beauty, like the Ugly Duckling, to find her beauty and bloom, but when she does she has a powerful presence and can be very influential in her world. Some assume she is high maintenance; they do that with exotic flowers, too. Even florists are sometimes uncomfortable raising the Bird of Paradise or the Protea, maybe because they take patience, but they do not need a lot of care. They do best left alone to flourish in warm, humid environments with fair soil. The Dramatic (of either kind) is like that, too. She has a drive for excellence that can be intimidating to more casual personalities. She also has a drive for popularity; but her independent nature is not patient with those who do not understand her, so she is often only close to a few friends that she really relates to. Her tight circle of friends is observed as a "click" because they are like an exotic hotel bouquet in a casual home. Unfortunately, they are often assumed to be a snob, yet they are the ones feeling snubbed for being "too much."

I have already related the Woman at the Well (who we called "Samaritan Barbie") to the Dramatic, but there is another woman from the Bible who illustrates this Img.ID very well: Hannah, the beloved first wife of Elkanah, whose second wife (Peninnah) was her rival. Like the Samaritan Woman, Hannah had a hard time with her peers.

A woman with the Dramatic Img.ID is often very respected in her community; sometimes that respect brings her fame, other times it brings her shame because she may make others feel intimidated around her. In either circumstance, she seldom realizes how influential she is. She is almost always a tall girl (unless this is her secondary clothing personality), and her height alone naturally exerts authority that she may very well be ignorant of because she can't relate to looking up to someone much taller than her.

She tends to have a majestic personality that attracts others, but it is hard for them to get to know her on an intimate level since she is so private. It takes a determined and confident person to pursue a healthy and lasting relationship with her unless she comes to understand that her independent nature makes others feel inadequate and she decides to consciously make herself available to them emotionally. Unfortunately, this girl is often the lonely one in a crowd. She has plenty of popularity, but few true friends. She longs to have intimate relationships to live her life with, but her impatience usually keeps her from taking the time to understand herself or others.

Dramatics love fashion and makeup and they tend to have a gift for doing creative things with excellence. Doing a makeover each morning is not a chore to these girls, it's something they enjoy doing, and they like to look beautiful. They have an eye for detail, so they tend to do the extras like eye shadow and liner and all the accessories. They also like their house and children to look beautiful, which sometimes comes across to others as controlling or obsessively concerned with other people's opinions, but that is not necessarily the case.

Dramatics don't bare their soul very easily; perhaps that is why they can be so misunderstood. Sometimes they are assumed to have it all together or to be full of wisdom, simply because they are spare with words. Other times they are misunderstood to be disapproving or snobbish, because though they may not be using their voice, their body language is very strong.

When these women do speak up they do it with such passion and drama that others listen intently (unless, of course, they go on and on, which is a way they sometimes hide from intimacy), but again they may be misunderstood to be very upset or extremely excited when inside they are simply stating facts (with flare!)

Look at Hannah for example. You find her story in 1 Samuel 1-2.

---　　✳ ✳ ✳　　---

Now there was a certain man of Ramathaim Zophim, of the mountains of Ephraim, and his name was Elkanah the son of Jeroham, the son of Elihu, the son of Tohu, the son of Zuph, an Ephraimite. And he had two wives: the name of one was Hannah, and the name of the other Peninnah. Peninnah had children, but Hannah had no children. This man went up from his city yearly to

worship and sacrifice to the Lord of hosts in Shiloh. Also the two sons of Eli, Hophni and Phinehas, the priests of the Lord, were there. And whenever the time came for Elkanah to make an offering, he would give portions to Peninnah his wife and to all her sons and daughters. But to Hannah he would give a double portion, for he loved Hannah, although the Lord had closed her womb. And her rival also provoked her severely, to make her miserable, because the Lord had closed her womb. So it was, year by year, when she went up to the house of the Lord, that she provoked her; therefore she wept and did not eat. Then Elkanah her husband said to her, "Hannah, why do you weep? Why do you not eat? And why is your heart grieved? Am I not better to you than ten sons?"
1 Samuel 1: 1-8

God had caused Hannah to be barren, which was a terrible stigmatism in her day. Most women can relate to the deep longing for a child, and many can relate to the consuming agony of waiting for conception. With each menstrual cycle the woman faces a very real grief. The longer infertility goes on the more life-consuming it is. Imagine adding to that personal struggle the brutal judgment of a society that believes you are cursed by God, and then add to that torment the worse kind of rival you could imagine: having your husband's other wife, who has had many sons and daughters, severely provoking you just to make you miserable (1:6). This was Hannah's life, and she couldn't get away from her rival; they shared the same residence, they traveled the same roads, they ate the same meals.

At one point (1:7) Hannah's heart was so sick she couldn't eat. Did anyone comfort her? No. Even her husband made it worse. He made her feel like she was unreasonable and ungrateful. He laid his words of guilt ("aren't I enough for you?") onto her already anguished heart (1:8).

Elkanah should have known Hannah best; he loved her. Yet he seemed to see her as a whiner and complainer who was more concerned about other people's opinion of her than of enjoying the life he was providing her.

What would a Dramatic do in that kind of a situation?

Cry.

Because she's a control freak?

No, because she is sensitive and passionate.

———— ✿ ✿ ✿ ————

So Hannah arose after they had finished eating and drinking in Shiloh. Now Eli the priest was sitting on the seat by the doorpost of the tabernacle of the Lord. And she was in bitterness of soul, and prayed to the Lord and wept in anguish. Then she made a vow and said, "O Lord of hosts, if You will indeed look on the affliction of Your maidservant and remember me, and not forget Your maidservant, but will give Your maidservant a male child, then I will give him to the Lord all the days of his life, and no razor shall come upon his head."

And it happened, as she continued praying before the Lord, that Eli watched her mouth. Now Hannah spoke in her heart; only her lips moved, but her voice was not heard. Therefore Eli thought she was drunk. So Eli said to her, "How long will you be drunk? Put your wine away from you!"

But Hannah answered and said, "No, my lord, I am a woman of sorrowful spirit. I have drunk neither wine nor intoxicating drink, but have poured out my soul before the Lord. "Do not consider your maidservant a wicked woman, for out of the abundance of my complaint and grief I have spoken until now." **1Samuel 1:9-16**

Dramatics tend to be very animated; that's why they do well in the fine arts. With their passionate nature they have a way of convincing you that their story is real. Because of their love for acting, sometimes reality can get blurry for them and they need someone to keep them in line with the truth. These women need to be careful that deception doesn't become an addiction, because they can get caught up in the power of changing someone's mind, or they may fall prey to a substance addiction in order to change their own mind in an effort to avoid reality.

But Hannah wasn't avoiding her reality; she couldn't get away from it. I believe she handled it in a way God would love all of us to: she sought Him for help. Maybe it was because there was enough drama in her situation; or perhaps it was because by then she had done all she could to try to control conception, and she had come to grips with the fact that final decision on this matter is God's. Maybe Hannah was controlling and manipulative in other areas of her life, that's a very real possibility, and maybe she was using her passionate nature in prayer with the purpose of manipulating God into giving her what she wanted. But I doubt it.

In Hannah's case, being very upset, it wasn't just her attitude that was misunderstood; her priest thought she was a drunk! (1:13)

I don't know about how you feel, but most of us have a really hard time with being misunderstood, especially if our character is being judged as unrighteous when our passion is to do good. Poor Hannah. She just wanted to have a baby. Dramatics want to take charge of their own life and live their dreams. It's hard for them to be held back by anyone, not because they are pushy control freaks, but because they are go-getters.

In fact, you will find that most Dramatics are business owners or professionals of some kind, because they are go-getters and they are very influential. But as we have talked about, whenever we have an ability to bear great influence in our world, our enemy will actively try to lead us astray. Satan tends to sidetrack Dramatics by making them blinded to their strength or leading them to be obsessed with it. Very often, even in a crowd of friends, this woman feels excluded or alone and she may not know why. People like to be around the Dramatic; she is fun. But she can be aloof because of her fear of being misunderstood and her independent nature, so as much as her friends love her, they tend to feel she doesn't need them, and so her relationships tend to be superficial or one-sided.

Dramatics who make a decision to guard their hearts, but still be vulnerable by making the first move in their relationships, are able to radiate balanced beauty in a way that is very inspiring to others.

If you are a Dramatic of either type, you are creative and influential. Your image should reflect who you are.

Your Motto: Straight-up modern and modest! *(Keep your lines straight, your fashion and quality high and be careful to remain relatable.)*

Suggestions: *You are a take-charge woman, who tends to get along just fine without anyone. People like you a lot, but often they think they have nothing to offer you … so they don't. Because of your strong will, you may rather drop a friendship than be the only one who puts in any effort, but if you make yourself vulnerable, you may find much greater joy.*

- Decide to be the one to make the first move in your relationships whether they are new or established.

- Another option: Become very patient while waiting for others to get the courage up to pursue you (or to apologize).

Your Wardrobe: *The body frame and structure of a Dramatic is extreme, just as her personality is. Your attire should make a statement, too:*
- High-fashion wardrobe; bold, trendy.
- Monochromatic outfits are a great look on you.
- Wear long, sleek lines.
- Choose only straight cuts; avoid curves.
- Tailored garments work well for you, only if severe.

Caution:
- Stay away from small, intricate and delicate details.
- Avoid curves and circles.
- Stay away from girly styles of any kind, especially lace and frills.
- Avoid mix-and-match separates (they'll only frustrate you and make you appear matronly)
- If you wear patterns, they should be bold and sweeping abstracts.

Shopping tips: *Find a store you love that carries the accessories as well as the clothing—or shop in malls. When you shop, finish the outfit (shoes, earrings, belts, etc.) while you have it with you, because most likely you will not wear it until it is complete anyway! Never skimp on accessories. Collect them (you probably already do!).*
- Focus on the accessories.
- If you need to cut costs, find base garments that you can wear with different accessories to make more outfits.

Your Fabrics:
- Fabrics should hold defined shapes.
- Softness is only appropriate if the lines are elongated and draping.
- Smooth, shiny fabrics are great, if placed appropriately on your figure.

Your Formal Attire: *Formal affairs are your thing. In fact, you are the host of most of them, and when you throw a party, you go all out! You don't mind dressing up at all; formal occasions are when you shine most. Do not play your style down. Enjoy who you* *are; but keep in mind that others may not know how to handle your dynamic presence. You must choose to make them feel comfortable around your beauty.*

- Your look is extravagant and detailed.
- Do not choose anything simple, small or cheesy.
- Great choices include anything bold, abstract, sweeping or geometric.
- Look for monochromatic coloring.
- Choose fabrics that hold a defined shape.

Your Accessories: *Sophisticated or artsy should describe anything you wear, and in your accessories is where it should shine. Sleek and elegant choices are best.*

- Choose bold, extravagant jewelry and accessories.
- Hats should be unusual and make a statement.
- Belts should be large, ornate and bold.
- Bags and shoes are best with angular shapes and straight lines.

Your Makeup: *You are the only clothing personality that can carry off heavy makeup without looking cheap, and you most likely enjoy wearing it. So have fun! Makeup is one of your best accessories.*

- Striking, dramatic style: use the eye and lip liners.
- Play up the eyes! Keep it sophisticated or artsy.
- You can wear any level of makeup well; just keep it appropriate for the event.
- Stay within your seasonal palette of colors.

Hairstyle: *Your look should be rather severe and sharp, head to toe. Have fun with your hair, but stay away from curly layers or soft, rounded shapes. Extremely long is great if your face can carry it. If you enjoy wearing your hair up, a great sophisticated look is a low, tight bun.*

- Sleek, geometric or asymmetrical cuts are great for you.
- Get creative with your hair color; you can afford the risk. But follow the rules for your seasonal palette when it comes to color:
    ◊ Winter or Autumn: solid colors.
    ◊ Summer or Spring: highlights or lowlights

Manicure: *Since having finished hands is very important to your look, you may want to consider false nails because they look nice so much longer. Whether you choose to keep*

them natural or not, spend the time or money to keep up your nails polished and clean.
Your manicures should be:

- Fashionably long in length.
- Square or somewhat pointed edges.
- Choose bold polish colors within your seasonal palette.
- When choosing nail art, choose lines, not frills.

CHAPTER TWENTY-ONE

CONFIDENT INGÉNUE

The Delicate Beauty

Ingénue

Generally, the Ingénue matures into a Romantic, sometimes during puberty, but sometimes it is not until midlife that they become sexy and alluring. Some Ingénues keep their fresh, youthful qualities and remain Ingénues all their lives.

Body type:
- Small-boned, but not necessarily petite.
- Dainty, often delicate in appearance.
- Naturally feminine.
- Gently rounded figure.
- Delicate frame.
- Average- to small-size hands and feet, with small wrist (shoe size less than 7; wrist size less than 6")

Facial features:
- Fine boned.
- Rounded cheeks and chin.
- Friendly, gentle eyes; usually large.
- Delicate coloring, in any seasonal palette.

Hair:
- Fine, often thin.
- May be straight or curly.

Character: *The Ingénue has a sweet, innocent nature that brings with it a quality of freshness that does not threaten others, but uplifts them and inspires them.*

This woman, like the flower I chose to represent her, may be small, but she is a breath of fresh air. The Ingénue, like the Baby's Breath, is the kind of beauty that completes those around her. The flower is often used to cover the stems and spaces in a bouquet. The Ingénue has a creative and complimentary nature that makes her friends all look and feel more beautiful when she is with them. She may appear to be dainty and delicate, but this woman is strong and sturdy, like the flower that is able to survive environments most flowers cannot endure. In fact, as long as this flower has a mostly-sunny environment and well-drained soil that is not acidic, the Baby's Breath can thrive and grow into great foliage that covers any area it is given. This young lady is like that: She will do whatever you need her to, and she will do it with joy. Unless she has poor soil. This beauty needs to be able to let the rain run off her back, so to speak, if her soil is too heavy and acidic, she cannot thrive, and in her desperation to survive she may not be able to bloom at all.

If I were to choose a woman from the Bible who best represents the Ingénue, I would choose Esther. This woman's story is so dynamic that there is a whole book, named after her and dedicated to telling the details of her life. She was a lovely young lady who lost her parents at a young age and was raised by her uncle, Mordecai. When the king set a decree that beautiful young virgins be gathered and brought into his quarters, Esther was chosen and taken from her land. She and the other girls who were collected were given beauty preparations for an entire year. During that time Mordecai kept a close watch on her, and those in charge of caring for her gave her extra favor.

Then the king's servants who attended him said: "Let beautiful young virgins be sought for the king; and let the king appoint officers in all the provinces of his kingdom, that they may gather all the beautiful young virgins to Shushan the citadel, into the women's quarters, under the custody of Hegai the king's eunuch, custodian of the women. And let beauty preparations be given them. Then let the young woman who pleases the king be queen instead of Vashti."

This thing pleased the king, and he did so.

In Shushan the citadel there was a certain Jew whose name was Mordecai the son of Jair, the son of Shimei, the son of Kish, a Benjamite. Kish had been carried away from Jerusalem with the captives who had been captured with Jeconiah king of Judah, whom Nebuchadnezzar the king of Babylon had carried away. And Mordecai had brought up Hadassah, that is, Esther, his uncle's daughter, for she had neither father nor mother. The young woman was lovely and beautiful. When her father and mother died, Mordecai took her as his own daughter. **Esther 2:2-7**

Ingénues have a special way of drawing out masculinity in a man. Even when they are fully matured they have a youthful and innocent way about them that naturally makes a man feel strong. Good men love to care for young ladies; it's part of God's design. His strength complements her tenderness; her sweet nature calls forth his strength.

Not all men are good, however. It seems to me that the mean men love the Ingénue as well; not because they want to fight for her, but they like to fight with her. Like a big brother picking on a young sibling just to prove his strength, a mean man wanting to look tough often sees the Ingénue as an easy target. She has a very inviting nature and is naturally willing to give all she has for those around her, and in her innocence she often falls victim to abuse. Unfortunately, unlike the Natural who reasons her way through difficult times, abuse not only rocks the world of an ingénue, it often changes her joyful, encouraging character. Where she is naturally enthusiastic for others, her passion becomes protective of herself—like a wounded dog. When this girl decides to "do it herself!" the essence of her beauty, her vulnerability, is robbed from her and she is left with an uncertainty about who she is.

Ingénues tend to have a hard time making decisions anyway, so when they are no longer sure of themselves—but determined to not need anyone else—they may push themselves away from others or they may become very compliant and simply follow the lead of anyone who tells them what to do (which can lead them back into more abuse).

This isn't how it happened with Esther. She was protected and cared for. Like a delicate flower, this Img.ID—when she is treated right, is a powerful beauty. Her tender and creative nature flourishes and accentuates the beauty of those around her, influencing them to be more of who they ought to be. That's what Esther did when she asked her people to fast and pray with her in order that she could save them from annihilation. She called forth their strength, and in turn they encouraged her.

———— * ❋ * ————

And Mordecai told them to answer Esther: "Do not think in your heart that you will escape in the king's palace any more than all the other Jews. For if you remain completely silent at this time, relief and deliverance will arise for the Jews from another place, but you and your father's house will perish. Yet who knows whether you have come to the kingdom for such a time as this?"

Then Esther told them to reply to Mordecai: "Go, gather all the Jews who are present in Shushan, and fast for me; neither eat nor drink for three days, night or day. My maids and I will fast likewise. And so I will go to the king, which is against the law; and if I perish, I perish!"

So Mordecai went his way and did according to all that Esther commanded him. **Esther 4:13-17**

Ingénues are team players. Sometimes they are overlooked (since they always look younger than they are, people assume they don't have much to offer) but when they step into the game, they bring the inspiration and the team wins. Esther's team won. If you haven't read it all, I suggest you do. It's a powerful story of God's great faithfulness coming through for His people.

The Ingénue's delicate frame and humble personality lends itself to beauty in balance. Her free temperament and youthful appearance commands adoration simply by her presence; if she guards her heart from becoming overly independent, or co-dependent, she can make a big difference in her world by encouraging others.

If you are an Ingénue, I encourage you to remember that God fights for you, even if others have fought with you; let Him heal your hurts and let your young, delicate beauty shine for His glory and not your own. Your image should reflect who you are.

Your Motto: Lighten up, girl; you're fine! *(Always choose light, girly, fine fabrics, styles and patterns)*

Suggestions:
* Remember God longs to fight for you; allow Him to, and don't let anyone steal your security. You have been clothed with strength and dignity by the only One who truly knows you.

Your Wardrobe: *Your look is light and crisp, and so your outfits must be sweet and creative like you. Simple feminine prints, floral patterns of all sizes make your good old-fashioned beauty come alive.*

- Victorian look is great on you!
- Choose soft, delicate feminine styles.

Caution:
- The weight of fabric should be your focus; avoid heavy fabrics or you will be lost in them.
- Be sure to finish your look with shoes, bag, coats and jewelry, or you may look too young and plain. This is where most Ingénues can be neglectful.

Shopping tips: *Quality is not crucial for you; you can get away with cheaper clothing and jewelry, and you can shop in the junior departments!*
- Choose your stores carefully to find your old-fashioned, feminine styles.
- Do most of your shopping in the Spring or Summer, since this is when the lighter weight fabrics are sold.

Your Fabrics: *Again, the weight of the fabric you wear is what is most important in your wardrobe; choose lightweight clothing such as:*
- Soft woolens, angora, cashmere.
- Fine silks and crisp cottons.
- Gauze or fine knits.
- Frilly frocks of tucks, ruffles and lace.

Your Formal Attire: *Your beauty radiates when you are dressed up because your look is very feminine. Short or long gowns or dresses are great on you; just be sure to keep the look young and innocent. Avoid anything bold or strong, or you will come across as a little girl playing dress-up. Choose:*
- Chiffons, organza or eyelet fabrics.
- Open crochet fabrics.
- Embroidered detailing.

Your Accessories: *You can economize your accessories, since there is a lot of costume jewelry that suits your style well. Expensive jewelry does not necessary look good on you; however, diamonds truly are your best friends! Some good choices are:*
- Small, dainty accessories of fair quality.
- Ornate fashion for evening wear.
- Delicate pearls.

- Floral ceramics, cameos.
- Ribbons, bows and flowers suit you well.
- Scarves are great accessories for you, whether around your neck, in your hair or on your shoes; just be sure they are lightweight.

Your Hairstyle: *Whatever you do with your hair, be sure it is feminine, soft and bouncy, like you.*
- If you like it curly, loose and light curls are best.
- If you prefer it straight, feather cuts will work well for you (especially if wearing it short).
- When you wear it up, be sure it is loose and flowing.
- Gentle tassels falling around your face and neck are a beautiful look on you.
- If you choose to color your hair:
  ◊ Be sure it is a soft look and follows your seasonal palette rules: (Autumn /Summer: Highlights and lowlights—natural looking, not chunky. Winter/Spring solid color—keep the color close to your virgin hair).
  ◊ Be sure to keep up with your color, no matter what you do with it, since showing roots does not suit your natural innocent look well.
  ◊ Be sure to book your next appointment before leaving the salon, so that you don't let someone else's needs get in the way of your own.

Your Makeup: *Your makeup should be delicate and luminous, very natural, simple and sweet, almost as if it were not there at all, although you do want to wear it, especially if your skin tone is uneven, as it only enhances your innocent beauty.*
- Winter/Spring: foundation and lip color/gloss.
- Summer/Autumn: foundation and mascara.
- Stay away from eyeliners.
- Choose eye shadows only if pale, neutral colors and well-blended.

Your Manicures:
- Medium to minimal length, rounded edges.
- Soft, light colors or French Manicure.
- Never ragged or unkept.

CHAPTER TWENTY-TWO

CONFIDENT ROMANTIC

The Glamorous Beauty

Romantic:

Body type:
- Average to short, rarely tall.
- Balanced figure, even if overweight.
- Shapely, soft, rounded, true figure 8.
- Busty, regardless of weight.
- Rounded hips with a waistline.
- Naturally feminine.

Facial features:
- Soft, rounded features.
- Large eyes.
- Feminine beauty.
- Rich coloring.

Hair:
- Fine, straight or curly.
- May be frizzy curls.
- May be thick or thin.

Character: *The Romantic woman is sensual in her appearance and in nature. She naturally gives great attention to the elements of taste, smell, touch and especially visual appeal.*

Like the orchid, this woman's beauty is luscious and captivating, but sometimes hard to bring to bloom. Orchids will not share their astonishing flowers with the world if they are not cared for properly. They need sun and water like any other flower, but caring for them is very intricate. They are a tropical flower that needs warmth but must have a change in climate or they will not bloom. They need to be in the sun but cannot take direct sunlight; they need to be watered slowly and precisely because too much or too little water will shut down their blooming. Some of them like to be root-bound in order to bloom; others like the freedom and drainage of a larger pot. You need to study this flower if you are going to succeed in drawing out its amazing qualities. The Romantic's beauty is delicate like that. Both the plant and the woman will endure poor conditions, but neither will share the beauty they have to offer. An Orchid will fill its pot with its large leaves and empty stems; the Romantic woman will fill her life with serving others but never really be able to offer her whole self because neglect causes her to shut down and stuffs away her own needs and desires.

If I were to choose a woman from the Bible who best represents the Romantic, I'd choose Tamar, the daughter-in-law of Judah. You find this woman in the book of Genesis, chapter 38. She was chosen to be the wife of Judah's son Er, who was a wicked man. When Er was killed for his wickedness, Tamar was given to Judah's next son, Onan, as was custom among the Jews. Onan was selfish and did not want to give his brother an heir; this displeased God so He took Onan's life from him. Judah was afraid of losing his third son, so he told Tamar to go back to her family and wait for him to get older... but then he never sent for Tamar.

Then Judah took a wife for Er his firstborn, and her name was Tamar. But Er, Judah's firstborn, was wicked in the sight of the Lord, and the Lord killed him. And Judah said to Onan, "Go in to your brother's wife and marry her, and raise up an heir to your brother." But Onan knew that the heir would not be his; and it came to pass, when he went in to his brother's wife, that he emitted on the ground, lest he should give an heir to his brother. And the thing which he did displeased the Lord; therefore He killed him also.

Then Judah said to Tamar his daughter-in-law, "Remain a widow in your father's house till my son Shelah is grown." For he said, "Lest he also die like his brothers." And Tamar went and dwelt in her father's house. **Genesis 38:6-11**

It is not unusual for Romantics to get pushed and pulled by others, especially men. Maybe it's because during their formative years they are Ingénues, maybe it's because they are so compassionate about others and so giving in nature that they believe others are gentle and generous too, or perhaps it is because they seldom put their own wants or needs ahead of others'. I don't know, but I have ministered to many Romantics who have been deeply wounded by others.

Romantics are full-figured women, or at least they have a curvy structure, very often a figure 8. I would say that about 75% of the Romantics I know developed their beautiful curves at a very young age. Some hit puberty when they are still children, although they are not the only Img.IDs that may develop young; for these girls, because they are sensitive emotionally, it becomes an issue. A Natural or Gamine who has boys gawking at her and girls cruel with jealousy toward her may say, "stupid kids!" but a Romantic feels things deeply and when the battle she is facing is a more mature issue than her years have granted her wisdom for, she makes vows to herself that are often very strong by the time she recognizes them.

For example, I have a friend who developed a great figure at age 9. Her girlfriends felt awkward around her, like they were left behind and she was too old to play with them, so they began excluding her. While girls paid less attention, boys paid more attention to herespecially the older boys, and we all know where that can lead. Her mother's worse nightmare came true. Someone she looked up to and should have been able to trust raped her. My friend vowed to never be vulnerable to anyone again.

I wonder if rape was the wickedness that Er was guilty of? Onan's sin toward her was quite the opposite: he wouldn't make love to her. Well, at least not completely. He did have his way with her. I'm not as explicit as God's Word, but you can read the details in verse 9. The point I want to make is that she must have been desirable, or he would have just let her live in his house untouched and pretended she was infertile.

Romantics are elegant, feminine women with flirty eyes and full lips, and a full bosom. Boobs are simply irresistible to some men. Right?

Let's keep going with the story. Eventually Judah loses his wife and Tamar waits while he goes through his time of mourning, but he still does not give the third son to her as a husband. When she hears he is making a trip to have his sheep sheared, she takes off her widow's clothing, puts a veil over her face and goes ahead of him to wait along the road he will travel. Clothing says a lot about the person wearing it. It always has, it always will. A veil meant she was available… if you know what I mean.

Now in the process of time the daughter of Shua, Judah's wife, died; and Judah was comforted, and went up to his sheepshearers at Timnah, he and his friend Hirah the Adullamite. And it was told Tamar, saying, "Look, your father-in-law is going up to Timnah to shear his sheep." So she took off her widow's garments, covered herself with a veil and wrapped herself, and sat in an open place which was on the way to Timnah; for she saw that Shelah was grown, and she was not given to him as a wife. When Judah saw her, he thought she was a harlot, because she had covered her face. Then he turned to her by the way, and said, "Please let me come in to you"; for he did not know that she was his daughter-in-law. **Genesis 38:12-16**

Tamar didn't offer herself, but Judah asked to have her for the night; and I'm sure that was her plan. Romantics are no fools. They have a certain power that comes with their kind of beauty. Their curvy figure, rounded features and gentle nature is captivating. We've talked about it all throughout this book: some women love that power, others hate it, many vacillate between both emotions.

Romantics vacillate.

Tamar may have been hiding her body in her widow's outfit; she may have determined in her heart to be content accommodating others while she waited for another husband. I bet she made her father's home a beautiful, comfortable place with all the details of lace, flowers, candles and music to make everyone feel at home while she was there. That's what Romantics love to do: comfort others. But again, they are no fools. Some people may assume they are because they can be manipulated into taking care of everyone else while neglecting themselves, but drive this girl too far and she will take care of herself, alright!

Tamar used one of her great assets—her figure—to go find what she needed: love and acceptance.

We all have that temptation as women, but it seems to me that just as the Romantic tends to feel compassion for others more deeply, she also feels her own emotions more deeply. Her vulnerability is part of what makes her so beautiful (it's also what makes her so great in public relations), but vulnerability is the thing she hates. She would accommodate nearly anyone's need, but she stuffs her own. She puts great emphasis on creating atmosphere, and has a very practical mind (which makes her a great nurse or hostess), but she seldom considers that her attitude toward herself can make others uncomfortable around her.

People are drawn to that which is authentic. It is hard to draw near to someone who is disrespecting herself even if she is showing you great love and respect.

One way Romantics can disrespect themselves is by flaunting their bodies. Our culture encourages it. They say, "If you've got it, flaunt it." Romantics may dress in a way that makes them come across as proud of their curves while at the same time speaking body language that says they are ashamed of themselves (especially if their figure includes rolls of extra curves). Whenever someone's actions say one thing and their attitude says another they may have a hard being trusted.

I believe Tamar was in that state of double-mindedness when she set out to meet her father-in-law. She was hiding from him, but she was teasing him with her availability. She had probably vowed to never need him, yet she was desperate to use him.

It is not uncommon that the see-saw the Romantic rides is with her weight. She may purposely or subconsciously put on weight to disuse her bosom with a belly, only to find her breasts and bottom are the main places she gains. So she tries to gain control by losing it all with diet and workouts, yet no matter how hard she tries, she just can't lose the pounds in the right spots.

Very often, in her efforts to gain control of her body, this woman ends up with an eating disorder that controls her. Or she may hide her figure in baggy sweatshirts and oversized clothes that only make her look dumpy. Why? Because, she has found that she is safest if others don't look at her! Besides, she would rather be busy taking care of others!

She may ride that emotional see-saw all her life unless she gives her frustrations to the One who created her.

Tamar must have shared her frustrations with God, because He blessed her abundantly. She not only became pregnant by her father-in-law, but with the birth of her twin sons, Tamar becomes part of the lineage of Jesus Christ. What a powerful witness to the faithfulness of God even in the midst of man's abuse and neglect.

The book of the genealogy of Jesus Christ, the Son of David, the Son of Abraham:

Abraham begot Isaac, Isaac begot Jacob, and Jacob begot Judah and his brothers. Judah begot Perez and Zerah by Tamar, Perez begot Hezron, and Hezron begot Ram. Ram begot Amminadab, Amminadab begot Nahshon, and Nahshon begot

Salmon. Salmon begot Boaz by Rahab, Boaz begot Obed by Ruth, Obed begot Jesse, and Jesse begot David the king. **Matthew 1:1-5**

If you are a Romantic, you work hard to make others to feel comfortable in your home or wherever you are; decide to make them comfortable around your image, too. That will only happen when you become comfortable with yourself.

- Recognize that your deep wounds come from your spiritual enemy, not from Man alone.
- Whether you have been withholding your beauty or forcing it, stop. Seek peace and pursue it.
- Allow yourself to be vulnerable again.

You are the epitome of femininity; your body was designed to draw others to you and to bring comfort. Don't let anyone take that from you by making you feel excluded or uncomfortable.

Your Motto: When you've got it, there's no need to flaunt it. *(Keep your look sophisticated and mysterious. Avoid thin, cheap or revealing wardrobe/accessories. Keep them guessing; your beauty is obvious, no need to flaunt it.)*

Your Wardrobe: *Your beauty is so strong that you do best to keep it simple. Choose feminine looks that don't reveal too much; your greatest power is in your mystery.*

- Choose rounded lines, soft curves.
- Choose loose, flowing outfits with a waistline, such as blousy tops and flowing skirts.

Caution: *The wrong outfit on you could easily make you look like a streetwalker. In fact, this is your seemingly endless frustration! And the revealing styles that are so popular today don't make it any easier for you!*

- Do not give away what you have too easily… but do not hide it either.
- Let your silhouette show your figure in a soft, gentle way (like your spirit is!).
- Don't be afraid to bring subtle attention to your hourglass figure; it's part of who you are!
- Don't forget to take into consideration how your Creator feels about you.

Shopping Tips: *The heart of most Romantics is not to flaunt her beauty; you may even have a hard time believing that you have beauty to offer, but the jealous eye does not understand that. Those without a full figure don't understand how careful you need to be with what you wear.*

- Balance is your key: keep it modest, but show it off.
- "If you've got it, flaunt it" is a death threat to your image.
- Don't work too hard at your image, keep your look soft and sweet, like your personality.
- Find the shop or boutique that suits your style; only shop there.

Your Fabrics: *Do not choose fabrics of poor quality, or your whole image will appear fake. If you need to cut costs, do it with your accessories because most costume jewelry looks great on you. Your finishes should be rich and luscious. Some good choices are:*

- Medium- to light-weight fabrics such as soft woolens, sweater knits, suedes and velvets. Stay away from heavy or bulky fabrics.
- Fluidity in all lines, head to toe.
- Draping, flowing fabrics with soft, ornate feminine lines.
- Oversized florals and polka dots or feathery shapes flatter you well; sharp or symmetrical lines and shapes do not.
- Avoid tailored, straight or horizontal lines and rough textures.
- Stay away from anything that hangs straight on you (especially big baggy sweatshirts!).
- Stay away from the revealing outfits that are too:
    ◊ Tight
    ◊ Low neckline
    ◊ Short hemline
    ◊ Lightweight fabrics

Your Formal Wear:
- Choose rich velvet, chiffon or lace dresses that cascade around your curves.
- Details such as sequins, rhinestones, lavish buttons, embroidery, etc., are great on you.
- For your more formal attire you may also want to choose silks or lace.

Do not show too much flesh, especially cleavage, or that will be all others see of you. Avoid anything tight and clingy or loose and baggy.

Your Accessories:
- Dainty in detail, but lavish in effect.
- Dressy look is ornate.
- Diamonds are very appropriate.
- Floral accents (in hair, corsage etc.).
- Silk scarves work well.
- Details such as sequins, rhinestones, lavish buttons, embroidery etc.

Your Hairstyle:
- Soft, rounded styles with a bounce.
- If long, soft curly layers are best.
- If short, feathered around the face is best.
- Avoid straight, blunt or stringy looks.

Your Makeup:
- Glamorous, sensuous, but not too heavy.
- Avoid eyeliner, but luscious lashes are great on you!
- You wear all levels of makeup well, except theatrical, as long as it is well blended and clean.

Your Manicures:
- Medium length with rounded edges.
- Fashionable colors, within your seasonal palette.
- Feminine nail art is nice on you, just don't overdo it.

CHAPTER TWENTY-THREE

CONFIDENT GAMINE

The Bold Beauty

Gamine

Body type:

- Short in height but sturdy.
- Small/petite to medium build.
- May be chunky or stocky.
- May be slender, but never fragile.
- Angular bone structure, unless also Romantic.

Facial features:

- Friendly, animated features.
- Small rounded cheeks and chin.
- Angular features if slim.
- Square jaw line.
- Often has turned-up nose.

Hair: *Most Gamines desire short hair unless influenced by someone they love. It may be:*

- Thick.
- Thin.
- Fine and straight.
- Coarse and curly.
- Any combination of the above.

Character: *The Gamine comes across as a very confident woman, because she has learned to stand tall though she is often towered over by her peers. She is very opinionated and has a way of persuading others to be of the same opinion; she is not afraid to say it like it is.*

The Gamine is much like the Calla Lilly; she is strong, sturdy and full of color and variety. The trumpet-shaped petals of the Calla Lilly are bright and bold and contrast with its thick leaves or any secondary color it may have. This flower can endure almost any condition; the more colorful it is the more it may need warmth, but the white ones bloom even in stormy, cold conditions. We need Gamines in this world; they thrive in situations where most of us would not know what to do. When they see crisis, they jump to action—like the flower that pokes through the ground before the rest of the plant. When the Calla Lilly does that, a new gardener might get the impression that something is wrong; when Gamines suddenly appear with their opinions or corrections, they may give off a first impression that doesn't accurately display their true nature. She may appear to be judgmental, but the truth is she is passionate about justice. Sometimes this woman's eagerness to fix things is like the Calla Lilly's fragrance (which isn't as appealing as most flowers), and people may step back from her, but she will always be admired, even if it's from a distance, because this woman's powerful presence is undeniable.

I have already shared with you that I liken the Gamine to Eve. I think she is a great example of this spunky woman who may be small in size but is large at heart. Eve was the mother of all mankind, and what a great role for this Img.ID! Gamines keep things in order; surely Eve was an organized woman or she wouldn't have been able to handle such a large family. Gamines make great mothers because they get involved in their kids' lives, and if discipline is needed they don't shy away from correcting. Although I must say it is not uncommon for a Gamine to be more blind to her children's errors than anyone else is.

Like Eve, the Gamine's passionate convictions may get her (or the entire human race!) in trouble at times, but it is that determination to correct things that makes a difference in this world. Perhaps Moses' mother would be a better example of a Gamine who followed her convictions and brought about good in her world.

———————— ❋ ❋ ❋ ————————

And a man of the house of Levi went and took as wife a daughter of Levi. So the woman conceived and bore a son. And when she saw that he was a beautiful child, she hid him three months. But when she could no longer hide him, she took an ark of bulrushes for him, daubed it with asphalt and pitch, put the child in it, and laid it in the reeds by the river's bank. And his sister stood afar off, to know what would be done to him.

Then the daughter of Pharaoh came down to bathe at the river. And her maidens walked along the riverside; and when she saw the ark among the reeds, she sent her maid to get it. And when she opened it, she saw the child, and behold, the baby wept. So she had compassion on him, and said, "This is one of the Hebrews' children."

Then his sister said to Pharaoh's daughter, "Shall I go and call a nurse for you from the Hebrew women, that she may nurse the child for you?"

And Pharaoh's daughter said to her, "Go." So the maiden went and called the child's mother. Then Pharaoh's daughter said to her, "Take this child away and nurse him for me, and I will give you your wages." So the woman took the child and nursed him. And the child grew, and she brought him to Pharaoh's daughter, and he became her son. So she called his name Moses, saying, "Because I drew him out of the water." **Exodus 2:1-10**

Moses was born during a time that Jewish boys were being thrown into the river to die. His mother would not comply to what she knew was wrong. This bold woman did follow the king's command; she did put her baby in the river of vicious alligators, but she did it her way. She made a waterproof basket for him and had her daughter follow Moses as he floated down the river to the arms of the king's daughter. When the princess found the baby, Moses' sister offered to get their mother to come and nurse the baby. That is a Gamine plan!

Gamines get things done.

Moses' mother hid him for three months before she put him in the river. Gamines are patient when they have a plan of action. I imagine that, during those months, this woman was not only planning but also working hard on the creation of that basket. Gamines don't stop to think about the work, and they don't care if you agree with them or not; if they feel something should happen they will do it immediately (or they will tell you to do it immediately).

I love Gamines. They are focused women who know how to have fun. Sometimes their focus makes them forget about fun, but when they let loose they are the life of the party (and they may then forget about the focus...) They are generally full of energy and multitalented. They are people-oriented, but sometimes assumed not to be, since their intense work ethic can override their people skills at times.

The Gamine does well in public relations where she can deal with people in groups more than individually, since her straight-up, to-the-point words are a bit too strong for the tender-hearted to hear directly, but are very helpful to hear generally. People are inspired by her energetic drive and charming personality, and because she has the boldness to deal with tender matters and has great enthusiasm for life and for others. She makes a great cheerleader, coach, lawyer or negotiator of some kind. She also does well in the medical field, because nothing embarrasses her and she loves the idea of wearing a uniform, since she seldom wants to dress up or think about what to wear.

She will dress up if she wants to and when she does her beauty comes alive, but she does not like to be pressured to be more formal or feminine. She also hates to be told she is cute, but because of her petite (but not frail) size and her animated features, she is adorable and people do tell her.

The Gamine who has her beauty in balance is a strong influence in her world.

If you are a Gamine, you are a woman in control, but full of fun and your attire should reflect who you are. Choose strong, bold, contrasting colors in outfits that hold their form. You are a compassionate, get-it-done kind of gal, be sure to put as much effort into showing your love for others as you do correcting what is wrong.

Your Motto: Do it, and forget it *(Your fun nature comes out more when you take a little time to look good, but your rebellious side tends to keep you from doing what it takes, especially if someone is telling you what to wear! Decide for yourself to put an effort into your image and then forget about it; if it's your own rule, you are still in control!)*

Suggestions:
- Realize that although you are quick-witted and have an eye for detail, not everyone else does—and they may not be judging you the way you think they are. You are your own worst critic.
- Be careful not to discard other's emotions with your matter-of-fact nature.
- Enjoy your friendships! Don't take life (and work) so seriously.

Your Wardrobe: *You are bold and sassy, and so should your clothing be (always include at least three colors, and keep it fun!)*
- Bright, contrasting, animated clothing of many colors brings out the best in you.
- Mix it up; wear mix-and-match outfits with some form and crisp color.

Caution:
- Be careful that your drive for life doesn't drive others away from your life.

Shopping tips: *When considering an outfit or store, think to yourself, "Does it say 'contemporary,' 'snappy,' or 'chic'?" (Also: "Do they have a petite section?") Shop only in those stores that do.*

- Choose outfits that are full of life and eye-catching detail.
- Look for garments that have straight sharp lines that are very tailored.
- Your necklines should be angular and your edges tailored or asymmetrical.
- Stay within your seasonal palette; that way each piece should mix-and-match with the ones at home.
- Choose one color to be your foundational color; accessorize with two to three more colors.
- Stay away from monochromatic and natural color schemes.
- Avoid rough textures.
- Choose outfits with crisp trims that contrast in color with the rest of the outfit.

Your Fabrics:

- Choose light-to-moderate weights that are defined in shape and easily tailored, such as oriental silks, crisp cottons and wool.
- The finish should be matte or low-luster with a smooth, refined surface.
- Your prints should be contemporary and full of life and color, just as you are.
- Avoid anything sheer, delicate, frilly, flimsy or intricate.

Your Formal Attire:

- Crisp metallics and beading.
- Sleek styles with tailored edges.
- Angular necklines, asymmetrical hemlines.

Your Accessories: *You may be happy to learn that a minimum amount of accessories is appropriate for the Gamine. Color is your best accent, whether it is in the jewels or in the shoes and belts. (Remember: Choose bold, contrasting colors within your seasonal palette.)*

- Simple, lightweight jewelry that is proportionate to your body size.
- Crisp geometric, asymmetrical or irregular shapes and details are your best options for all your accessories.
- Stay away from antique or artisan styles.

- Scarves are not "your design"—give them to your Dramatic and Romantic girlfriends.
- For shoes, you will do best in low heels and loafers.

You are really the only personality who can wear hosiery that contrasts with your hemline. In fact it's a great staccato look for you. If you choose dark hose, be sure it is sheer.

Your Hairstyle: *You may have straight or curly hair (by genetics or by chemistry); whichever way you wear it, keep it simple—spunky, but simple. Short, cropped boyish cuts look great on you! Whatever length you choose, find a style that is spunky and alive; don't let your energy be sapped by something boring!*

- Casual, wash-n-wear style.
- Best if short, bouncy, fun.
- If long, must have style with flair of fun:
  ◊ One length with a straight bottom line.
  ◊ Lots of layers all over that fringe the face.
  ◊ Spunky bangs.

Your Makeup: *You may not care to wear makeup, but when you do you become more alive. You may find it worth taking the time each day to do a five-minute makeover. Do it and forget it!*

- Keep it defined, fresh and animated.
- Wear a foundation and do eyes or lips:
  ◊ Winter/Spring: define the lips with color (plus liner for formal events).
  ◊ Summer/Autumn: Define the eyes with liner and mascara, (plus shadow for formal events).

Your Manicures:

- Short to medium length.
- Softly squared edges.
- Colorful polish.
- Fun, but simple nail art.

CHAPTER TWENTY-FOUR

CONFIDENT KNOWING YOUR PERSONAL IMG.ID

Confidence is Knowing Who You Are

Now that you have read about the six variations of feminine beauty, are you confident about which one (or maybe two) you are?

When assessing a group of women I almost always have someone who is not quite sure which clothing personality she is. Most often this is because she is a combination of two, but sometimes it is simply because she is one personality who would rather be, or was taught to be, another personality. This is often the case for Gamines (who do not change their minds easily, so they tend to stay loyal to whichever personality influenced them growing up) and for Ingénues (who tend to follow the rules they know, without really even considering how they feel about them).

If you have taken the image assessment test and read through the chapters on each Img.ID, but are still unsettled on which one you are, I encourage you to read on.

You don't need to understand clothing personalities to know when something you are wearing is a really bad choice for you. You may have had this experience when you tried something on that, though you loved it on the rack, you felt awkward or uncomfortable wearing it and you knew right away that the outfit was simply "not you." Understanding the various styles helps ensure that the money you spend on your hair, wardrobe and accessories is invested into building your confidence versus draining it.

So what is "you"?

What makes you feel confident, empowered and beautiful? Perhaps you are surprised that not all the fashion rules you are following are inappropriate for you. Stepping out of the fashion box you have always obeyed may be like breaking out of a cocoon, but it may bring you just the freedom you need to make your beauty radiate. It's time to let go of what the fashion police think; their rules don't suit all styles. You are your own person, and your image needs to follow your Personal Image Identity, not Joan Rivers'.

Your Personal Img.ID includes your sizes, shapes and proportions as well as your personality and preferences. In general, your Img.ID takes the name of your clothing personality, which may be one style or a combination of two.

Some image combinations will create contradictions that you may need to work out so that your image represents you well. We will go over that. It is strong inconsistencies between who you are and what you wear that you need to avoid; bending rules that do not defy your character is fine. Follow your Img. ID guidelines like you do the white-dashed centerlines when driving; cross them only when necessary and safe, otherwise you may find yourself way off course. Fashion rules are meant to guide you in accentuating your beauty; they are not meant to control you any more than traffic rules are. You can get to where you want to go without remaining within the street lines, but you sure have a better chance of getting there without doing yourself any harm if you do. Disregarding Img.ID guidelines may not cause safety issues, but following them will keep you from making choices that may breed confusion, insincerity and mistrust in others toward you.

Take Susan Boyle's 2009 audition with "Britain's Got Talent," for example. When she said she wanted to be like Elaine Paige, the audience rolled their eyes and snickered at her. No one believed in her. Why? Susan knew she could sing and she was excited to be on that stage. Confidence wasn't the gifted singer's issue, beauty was.

That now-famous contestant did what so many of us do on a regular basis: she made image choices that she liked, but not necessarily ones that liked her. Dressing according to opinions (our own or someone else's), without considering whether we are representing ourselves well is foolish. So is letting poor clothing choices draw all the attention away from the impression we want to portray.

It wasn't that Susan Boyle didn't try to look beautiful for her important day; she did dress up. But her image was competing with her personality; making her look like a phony who was trying to be someone she was not. She is a bold beauty (Gamine), but her lacy dress was Romantic. Her sling-back shoes were Classic. Her wash-and-wear hair, bushy eyebrows and plain necklace were Natural. I believe that her confusing image sent a subconscious message to her audience that she was confused and fake, and this is what made so many people laugh at her. It may be commonly said that we can't judge a book by its cover, but we do, so let's each be sure that our "cover" represents us well.

Your Personal Img.ID:

You are unique.

While other women may have similar coloring, facial shapes and features, figure frame, height, weight and proportions as well as identical clothing personality or personal preferences as you have, no one else will have the same combination of all of these things that you have. That's why your Img.ID is personal.

An image assessment does not put you in a box. It sets you free from one.

Knowing your style and its greatest assets as well as knowing your imperfections and how to best balance them may seem like generalized regulations but remember, this does not take away from your individualism any more than the florist's assessment of her various flowers does. Appreciate your own beauty just as you appreciate each flower in a bouquet. Even a vase full of the same kind of daisies brings a variety of beauty. No two individuals, even if they are the same style, are alike.

Enjoy that about yourself. Enjoy that about others. The root of all unhappiness is comparison.

Be who you were designed to be:

- If you are a **Classic** beauty, who wants things done properly, then be proper in all that you do and all that you wear, and don't let others make you feel badly about that. You are needed; do not let your independence rob you of the joy of needing others.

- If you are a **Natural** beauty, who wants things done casually, then be simple in all that you do and all that you wear, and don't let others make you feel like you are less. You are inspiring and inviting; allow others to inspire you, too.

- If you are a **Dramatic** beauty, who wants things done excellently, then be passionate in all that you do and all that you wear, and don't let the judgment of others make you feel foolish. You are a powerful influence; be careful not to be intimidating.

- If you are an **Ingénue** beauty, who wants things done peacefully, then be gentle and sweet in all that you do and all that you wear, and don't let others rob your peace. You complete others; let them complete you, too.

- If you are a **Romantic** beauty, who wants things to be pleasing, then be luxurious in all that you do and all that you wear, and don't let other people's poor character shut down yours. You bring others comfort and healing; be sure to allow yourself the same.

- If you are a **Gamine** beauty, who wants things done right, then be bold and colorful in all that you do and all that you wear, and don't let your passionate work ethic rob the joy from your relationships. Your strength is needed; do not hide it, but don't force it, either.

- If you are a combination of any of these beauties, you may find that there are times when you are not quite sure what you want; this is not unusual. In fact it is very common for Christian women who have been taught to "die to self" to be unsure of what they really want for themselves (in life and in wardrobe!). This was the problem I had, and I encourage you, if this is the problem you have, then take the time to work out any areas where your priorities or choices may conflict, so that you can be confident and consistent, being your true self.

Combination clothing personalities:

The following advice is for those with combination personalities. These combinations are especially common for the strong personalities (Classic, Dramatic, Gamine) with soft coloring (Summer, Autumn) or for the soft personalities (Natural, Ingénue, Romantic) with strong, contrasting coloring (Winter, Spring).

You may also find this advice helpful for mother/daughter relationships.

In fact, if you were raised by a woman with a different personality, you may find that her influence shows itself as your secondary personality. This is not wrong; this is part of who you are. You may be aware that certain plants produce different colors blossoms according to the soil they are grown in. Your upbringing is the soil in which God chose to plant you so that your development would be what He could use for His glory.

- **Classic / Natural:** The Classic's desire to have things done properly may conflict with the Natural's desire for things to be casual and comfortable. If you are a combination of these two clothing personalities, you may feel pulled in two directions at times, but if you allow them to balance each other out, your wisdom and grace can be extremely inspiring. Sometimes you may need to choose areas that you let yourself (and others) be casual about while in other areas you remain faithful to the rules. As for your wardrobe: Choose ensemble dressing of the Classic, with soft-tailored influences and textures of the Natural. Avoid mix-and-match.

- **Natural / Classic:** This same combination, when the Natural beauty is strongest, may be even more prone to self-contempt. The laidback nature of the Natural may win most inner battles, but the passion for proper professionalism may rob the joy from quiet time with its guilt. My advice is to use your desire to be more social to motivate you to get your tasks done first, and then when work time is over enjoy the people in your life. As for wardrobe: When casual, choose sporty Natural styles. Focus on fabric textures in place of accessories. Choose carefree hairstyles, but keep them tidy. For more formal wear, follow Classic guidelines.

- **Classic / Dramatic:** Both of these personalities are very independent; if this combination is you, be careful not to shun others, allow them to be involved in your life whether you need them or not. The Classic tends to be somewhat reserved, whereas the Dramatic is rather emotionally sensitive. This is where you may struggle; allow yourself to be strong when you feel strong, but do not be ashamed of what you feel. Desiring to have things done properly and excellently can be overwhelming for others and exhausting for you; continually grow in grace for others and for yourself.

As for your wardrobe: Choose Classic styles with bold finishes; focus on refined details with choice accessories. Be sure to update your wardrobe when needed.

- **Dramatic / Classic:** While the emotional battles that this combination fights may be similar to that of the Classic/Dramatic, if your strongest personality (your physical makeup) is the Dramatic, you may be more likely to take offenses personally; be especially careful not to shut down on others. Realize that the rejection you feel may often be simply because your strength and wisdom can be intimidating to others. As for your wardrobe: Choose high fashions with elegance of good quality. Highly accessorize. Allow yourself to shop!

- **Classic/Ingénue:** Technically, this combination doesn't really exist except for the years of transitioning to the Classic/Romantic. The Classic is mature in features, physique and personality, whereas everything about the Ingénue is youthful and should be. If you feel this is you, follow Classic guidelines, being sure to keep your look soft and feminine; but don't dress or act younger than you are or you may come across as insincere. Your wisdom and professionalism is needed and is nothing to be ashamed of. Be and let be.

- **Ingénue / Classic:** If this combination is the other way around, and you are more of a Ingénue beauty with Classic influences, then the maturity factor does not have to compete. In fact, these two clothing personalities can complete each other. The compassionate and creative Ingénue personality blends beautifully with a strong and wise Classic temperament. And a young lady acting mature is much easier to believe than a mature woman acting youthful. The challenge can be dressing the part because the Classic look tends to drain this delicate beauty. For casual wear, follow Ingénue guidelines. For more formal wear, choose Classic looks with soft feminine features. Whether dressing up or not, pay careful attention to the weight of fabrics, being sure anything you wear is soft, feminine and flowing.

- **Classic / Romantic:** Both of these personalities tend to guard their vulnerability, but if you are a combination of the Classic and Romantic (with either as the primary personality), and you are willing to risk sharing yourself, you have a lot to offer your world. A Classic woman with Romantic influences may find that her desire for proper and professional details is complicated by her desire to have things esthetically pleasing. If this describes you, be careful not to let your drive for details overwhelm you or others. Instead, allow your compassion for others to complete the areas where you may be more task-oriented and do not let your sensitive side stop you from doing great things. As for wardrobe: Choose Classic styles except the tailoring; choose Romantic finishes and accessories.

- **Romantic / Classic:** If your physical attributes are more Romantic but the Classic influence is strong, you may find your desire to please others can sometimes hinder you from doing what you know you should, or you may find that your passion to help others can keep you from helping yourself. But, if you can keep your attention to detail balanced with your deep concern for others, you may find that your combination of wisdom and compassion is a precious commodity and your influence is invaluable. As for your wardrobe: Choose feminine fabrics and Classic styling, especially curved and fitted silhouettes; avoid boxy styles.

- **Classic / Gamine:** The combination of these two personalities is quite rare because it is not just the nature of one that is quite opposite the nature of the other. The physical attributes of a Classic are well balanced and proportionate as well as average. The physical attributes of the Gamine, on the other hand, are usually animated and extraordinary. If you feel you are this combination, more than likely you were raised by a Gamine. Choose Classic styles but be sure the colors are bold and that you have at least three contrasting colors in every outfit. Avoid animated clothing or accessories.

- **Gamine / Classic:** These two personalities are each productive, powerful and task-oriented. If you are a combination of these two, be careful that your independent nature and strong work ethic do not rob you from meaningful relationships. You are a highly influential woman, so be sure to earn the respect your presence commands. Be careful that your desire for comfort doesn't drain your image; your proper nature needs to show in your attire. Avoid the ensemble dressing of the Classic, but choose Classic lines and cuts, just mix and match them. Be sure to add lots of contrasting color, a signature of the Gamine style.

- **Natural / Dramatic:** The Natural beauty wants to be comfortable and casual, while the Dramatic beauty has no problem sacrificing these things for fashion and excellence. If you are a combination of these two personalities, you may be well aware of the conflict this arouses in your own wardrobe, especially when you need to dress up. Be careful not to overdo your fashion statements or others may feel you are putting on a show. Follow the Natural guidelines first, being sure to keep your image relatable and inviting, then add accessories like the Dramatic. Have fun with Dramatic makeup if you want, but be sure it is not too harsh; keeping the colors soft will allow you to wear heavy makeup without it overpowering your casual side.

- **Dramatic / Natural:** If your primary personality is Dramatic and you prefer the casual nature of your Natural side, you might not yet have discovered the joy of fashion. I encourage you to step out into the makeup and accessory world; you may just find that your beauty comes alive with a little eyeliner and bling. Choose chunky, bold accessories in order to keep your style somewhat casual. As for your wardrobe: Choose contemporary designs and lines, especially if elongated, oversized or novelty. Remember the texture of Natural, but not necessarily the mix-and-match; monochromatic looks that are casual and textured are a great option for you.

- **Natural / Ingénue:** These two personalities make a beautiful combination: casual and peaceful. Talk about inviting! If this is you, don't let your carefree nature keep you from making an impact in your world because you have much to offer. Be sure to step out of your comfort zone and share your gentle, creative side. As for your wardrobe: Follow Natural guidelines, focusing on textured fabrics that are not too stiff or heavy. Choose feminine styles and features.

- **Ingénue / Natural:** If you feel you are this same combination but Ingénue is your primary personality because of your physical traits, then more than likely it is your only personality. An Ingénue may be drawn to the peaceful choices of the Natural, because she, too, is nonthreatening. But being too casual in wardrobe, or in life, only drains the beauty that an Ingénue has to offer. Follow the Ingénue guidelines, being sure to bring out your femininity.

- **Natural / Romantic:** This is another truly beautiful combination of personalities: casual and glamorous; carefree and caring. There may be times when it is hard to blend these qualities, but it can be done. There is something very powerful about a woman who isn't overly concerned with herself or others, but cares deeply for them. If this combination is you, risk getting involved in other people's lives, your expressed concern may be just the validation they need. As for your wardrobe: Find quality clothing that follows the Natural guidelines and are softly feminine; country–western influences may be a great option for you.

- **Romantic / Natural:** This same combination in reverse presents a different challenge: having more sensitive feelings with a desire to make them no big deal and having a glamorous body with a desire to be casual or sporty. These contradictions need to be handled carefully. If you feel this combination is you, more than likely you were raised by a Natural whom you respected. Please know that although others may not feel things as intensely as you do, your emotions are not wrong and they are needed. Even the most callused person can find healing when someone else sheds a tear for them. Be passionate; it is who you are. Be and let be. As for wardrobe: Follow the Romantic guidelines and let your mom follow the Natural ones.

- **Natural / Gamine:** If your physical attributes are like those of a Natural and you have a strong personality, then you may be this combination. But if you are not tall and you have any of the Gamine physical attributes (especially the animated facial features) then you may not be a Natural at all. Gamines tend to desire a casual lifestyle and comfortable clothing, but following the Natural image guidelines can completely drain their beauty. I know this might rile you, but if it does this is another confirmation that you are a Gamine. More than half the Gamines I have assessed think they are Naturals. A Natural beauty seldom prefers a bold lifestyle unless she had a Gamine mom and in that case she is compromising her true self. A casual beauty should not follow the Gamine guidelines, because she will feel awkward and phony. Again, be and let be.

- **Gamine / Natural:** The reverse combination is possible and is quite beautiful because these two personalities can balance each other out. If you have Gamine attributes and prefer a peaceful, non-confrontational lifestyle, then follow Gamine guidelines of crisp, staccato and contoured outfits to accentuate your beauty. Bring in the casual side by avoiding the unstructured styles but including the texture of the Natural. If you have a strong passion to make sure life is fair for those you love, then the Natural preference you have chosen may actually be more Gamine than you think. Consider letting go of certain choices that may squelch your true, spunky personality.

- **Dramatic / Ingénue:** Both of these personalities are strong and sensitive, making them very much alike. Yet they are very different. The Dramatic tends to be sensitive inside but she shows herself strong, whereas the Ingénue wears her heart on her sleeve but has amazing resilience in overcoming difficulties. This combination needs to be especially careful that she lives a life true to who she really is. If you are a tall, exotic beauty with a youthful nature and desire for feminine looks, this may be you. Keep in mind that your passionate nature may be intimidating to some and misunderstood by others. Guard your heart with all diligence, because your animated and creative nature brings life to those around you, whether they appreciate it or not. Focus on Dramatic guidelines, but be careful to keep your wardrobe light and youthful.

- **Ingénue / Dramatic:** If your physical attributes suggest the delicate beauty of the Ingénue but your preferences are mostly Dramatic, then you may find yourself very frustrated with people who treat you like a child, or look down on you as if you are trying to be someone you are not. The strength and maturity of an Ingénue is commonly missed in first impressions because of her youthful appearance, but throw in the powerful nature of a Dramatic and no wonder you are misjudged at times. I'm afraid this may be your cross to bear; you would do well to make it a challenge you enjoy. Give people grace; they are only human. If you let their insulting ways take a bitter root in your heart, it will destroy your sweet and gentle nature. As for your wardrobe: Follow the Ingénue guidelines, accessorizing like the Dramatic, but be sure that anything you wear is delicate and feminine or the Drama will come across as overpowering and phony.

- **Dramatic / Romantic:** This combination of personalities makes a great ministry leader. The Dramatic nature is very inspiring and is willing to take charge to do what is needed, while the Romantic nature cares deeply for others. If this is you, be careful not to let your sensitive side overrule your great strengths. People expect a lot from those who lead; do not let the offenses get to you. Determine to be an over-comer and God will use you for great things. As for wardrobe: Choose high-fashion looks with feminine details such as elaborate buttons, beads, accents and accessories.

- **Romantic / Dramatic:** Women with a Romantic physique seldom prefer the Dramatic lifestyle unless they had a Dramatic feminine influence that they would like to emulate. The Romantic nature tends to need her time alone whereas the Dramatic loves a party. If you feel you are this combination, you may find yourself exhausted trying to keep up with yourself. I encourage you to consider if the busy life is really what you want, and if it is not, let it go. Be and let be. As for wardrobe: Follow Romantic guidelines, avoid the straight lines and high-fashion looks of the Dramatic, but enjoy accessorizing with feminine options.

- **Dramatic / Gamine:** Here's a powerful combination: excellence and justice. Wow, this woman can get things done! If you are this tall, exotic, spunky girl who is unafraid of fighting for what is just, keep in mind that your strength can be intimidating, or it can be influential. At times your attitude will determine which you are; other times you have no control over how others receive you. Do your best anyway and when others reject you, love them anyway. Don't shut down or cast out of your life the people who hurt you; give them time to understand you. Your strength should not be deterred by anger. As for wardrobe: Always choose high-fashion looks with lots of color, head to toe. Be sure to accessorize, but most of all Wear Your Smile. Be the first to say "hi" or others may be too intimidated to approach you.

- **Gamine / Dramatic:** If you are a shorter version of this same combination, you may be less intimidating but just as powerful. Use your strength for good, being careful not to put work before relationships, and God will use you for great things. As for your wardrobe: Choose clothing that holds its shape, not loose or oversized. Geometric or asymmetric styles with lots of color are best.

- **Ingénue / Romantic** and **Romantic / Ingénue:** Every Romantic was once an Ingénue. If you feel you are either of these combinations, you are probably in transition or have become a Romantic but still want to hold onto the little girl inside you. The desires of each of these personalities are very similar; they both care deeply for others and are very creative, but when they are wounded they respond differently (see the chapters on each of these personalities). This, and the difference in their figures, determines how they dress. If you have a youthful, petite figure: Follow the Ingénue guidelines. If you have a full figure: Follow the Romantic guidelines.

- **Ingénue / Gamine:** The strong, sturdy nature of a Gamine can blend well with the sweet, delicate nature of an Ingénue, if this woman is careful not to take offense with others. If you have the youthful physique and the bold nature of this combination, you may have been raised by a Gamine. I encourage you to search your soul for your true desires. If you feel overwhelmed trying to be strong when you would rather be sweet, then maybe it's time to let go of the expectations others have placed on you. Be and let be. If you believe this combination is truly you, then follow the Ingénue guidelines, being sure to wear bold colors.

- **Gamine / Ingénue:** Again, this combination is possible, but most likely the secondary personality is another woman's influence on you. If you have Gamine characteristics and truly desire to be more gentle and sympathetic with others, then follow Gamine guidelines with Ingénue influences. Choose fitted styles in medium- to light-weight fabrics that have soft, feminine details like lace, bows or floral prints. If you feel you want to make a change, and become more bold and decisive, then consider letting go of the timid side. Don't let anyone stop you from being who God called you to be. We need strong women who will fight for others in this world. Let's say it together: Be and let be.

- **Romantic / Gamine:** I see this combination often, and when this woman comes to understand herself she is very much like the butterfly emerging from its cocoon. The Romantic woman's sensitive spirit is truly beautiful when she has the Gamine nature to protect it and drive it to do good. To facilitate that she must allow herself to forgive the disappointments and failures in her life; otherwise, the Gamine nature will guard her cocoon and keep her shut out from the world. If this is you, I encourage you to seek healing and allow God to use your amazing character, which cares deeply for others and is willing to fight for them. Fight for yourself, too, but be careful not to inflict your pain onto innocent bystanders. As for wardrobe: Follow Romantic guidelines being sure to add bold, contrasting colors and fun, animated and geometrical patterns.

- **Gamine / Romantic:** If your physical traits are more like the Gamine, but you have a sensitive and compassionate spirit, then you, too, have a beautiful balance to your character. More than likely, you are already doing something good with your life. Keep at it; there is great reward in serving others. The challenge for you may be in finding attire that suits you well. My experience with most women of this combination is that they prefer simple and comfortable clothing, which is neither bold nor glamorous, in order to keep a low profile. I recommend that you step out of your comfort zone, and be as bold with your wardrobe as you are with your personality. Follow Gamine guidelines, choosing fabrics and prints that are crisp, formed, animated and fun. Be sure there is a feminine flair to everything you wear and see if you don't feel more confident and beautiful.

Confidence is Knowing Whose You Are

As we come to the conclusion of this book, I pray that you have learned a great deal about yourself—body, mind and soul—and that you are now confident about your reflection of the One who made you. My hope is that you care for yourself inside and out without focusing on outward beauty and neglecting inward beauty or focusing on inward beauty so much that you neglect the outward appearance that validates what you have to offer. You now know *personally* "what not to wear" so that your image efforts will be far more efficient and you won't waste your time trying to achieve a look you may love but that is simply "not you."

But confidence conflicts will still arise.

Some days, self-consciousness, embarrassment or shame may try to get the best of you. Other days, pride or self-centeredness may creep in. But just as a tightrope walker may wobble from time to time, you can maintain balance if you keep a proper perspective of your purpose, power and priorities. Grow in grace for yourself and for others. You are not alone in this world; others need you and you need others. Never let the beauty battle separate you from the love of God or from loving others with God's love. BE and LET BE.

Each of us has a cross to bear, and we will deal with it according to our faith, our past experiences and our personality. At times our emotions will set us off-priority; we need to cast our cares on the Lord and do our best to continue our calling with character. Other times circumstances will rock our assurance and we will need help; we need to accept it with gratitude and look forward to the days when we can offer it to someone else. Sometimes temptations will wrap a tight grip around us and we cannot shake the shame they leave us; we need to humble ourselves and repent and realize that experiencing unconditional love is the truest source of confidence.

Actually, this is the final thought I want to offer you before closing this book: **Unconditional love is the truest, most powerful and lasting source of confidence.** It doesn't wear off like makeup does; no, not at all. Unconditional love changes us in a way that other trials and temptations may try to undo, but those conflicts are what wear off. In the end, women (and men) who know they are loved unconditionally are the ones who are truly confident beauties.

Is that you, my friend? Have you really taken this all to heart, or has this been just another interesting reading experience?

———— * ❋ * ————

Do you know that the very hairs on your head are numbered? They are. Are not two sparrows sold for a copper coin? And not one of them falls to the ground apart from your Father's will. But the very hairs of your head are all numbered. Do not fear therefore; you are of more value than many sparrows. **Matthew 10:29-31**

Let's think about this amazing fact for a moment, because it is proof of the unconditional love your Heavenly Father has for you and I believe it will seal your confidence—a sort of fairy dust for your new beautiful wings.

The fact that the very hairs of your head are all numbered is found in Matthew 10:30, and it is written in red lettering, which means these words are spoken directly from the lips of Christ. I always considered this verse very powerful. After all, even as a hairdresser, with all my clips and combs I don't think I could ever count any client's follicles! I love the thought of God keeping track of how many hair strands each of us have. I just picture Him keeping a running tab as each of us lose and regain multiple strands over the course of our days.

But what our Lord is saying is so much more than Him keeping count of our locks.

I'm sure you learned a bit about DNA in school, just as I did. The amazing double helix structure carries biological information of living organisms from one generation to the next. DNA is not just 20,000 genes on 23 pairs of chromosomes; it is loads of information about who you are and what your heritage is. It's not just which attributes you get from which parent, it's what you eat and what they ate, and so much more. Your DNA contains your Img.ID and everything about your personality, including how you respond to confidence conflicts and why.

The information in DNA is stored as a code, which can be interpreted as numbers. Now think of what Jesus was saying.

God knows the very numbers of your hair. He knows your DNA.

You might be saying, "Yes, of course He does, He's God!" But do you know that if you took that code and wrote it down on both sides of as much paper as you needed and then stacked those papers on top of each other, that the pile would go to the moon and back many times?

It would.

And that's how deep and high His love is for you. Unconditional love is not always warm and fuzzy; but it is truly intimate. God knows every intricate detail about you and He has a purpose for your life. If He cares that deeply about you, and you fail or others hurt and disappoint you, do those common life experiences hold any weight in comparison?

It makes me think of the book I used to read to my children. Maybe you read it to yours: "To the Moon and Back," by Randi M. Hull. It's a story of the constant and unwavering love between a mother and her child. As the child grows the mother wonders if her daughter will ever know how much she is loved.

I wonder if we could ever know how deeply we are loved by our perfect God?

I think of the times my children have been hurt and how sweet a reward it is to know they found comfort in my arms. I cherish the times they have messed up and come to me for forgiveness and were able to move on and try again. I get teary-eyed thinking of the days they put their disputes behind them and simply, joyfully played together with no grudges held. I wonder if they will ever know that they could do no wrong that would take my love from them.

Yet I am selfish and prideful and so often I claim their lives as my achievement and try to make my agenda their responsibility. God does not do that to us.

He wants us to enjoy our lives and to walk in peace and triumph. Period. No strings attached.

I am ready to do that. Are you?

If you are, then would you pray this prayer with me?

Dear God, help us to trust in your unconditional love. Thank you for loving us even though we are full of imperfections and failures.

Forgive us for trying to prove ourselves, and help us to seek only Your approval. Forgive us for trying to live in our own strength, and help us to humbly accept Yours. Forgive us for trying to control our circumstances and to manipulate others; help us to relinquish control to You and increase our faith. Forgive us, God when we have held grudges or shut down our spirit on others; we do not want to be angry or bitter people, we want to seek peace and pursue it. Help us to speak up when we need to and clearly make our heart known; help us to fight for what is right and to bring to You in prayer any battle that ought not be fought out in the world.

Thank you, God, for showing us that beauty may be fleeting and can easily become prideful, but is not wrong. Help us to find balance with our image every day. We want to be beautiful to you. We want to be confident and inviting. Help us to take care of ourselves without focusing on ourselves. Thank you for appreciating beauty; help me to appreciate it, too—even my own beauty. I don't want to compare myself with others anymore. You are the Supreme Stylist and I accept your design of the body you gave me. I want to be who you desire me to be, and I want to let others be who you designed them to be. For your glory, Lord, not my own. Amen.

Thank you for spending this time with me, I only wish I knew you personally. But now it's time for you to go, soar with confidence and beauty and bring the people in your world the same kind of comfort and joy that they feel when they are surprised with a glimpse of a butterfly fluttering amongst the flowers.

ABOUT THE AUTHOR

 Author and speaker, Catrina Welch, began her career as a cosmetologist right out of high school and soon after furthered her education and became an image consultant. Helping women look good is only a small part of her life's work; Catrina's greatest passion is helping women overcome image issues so they can feel good about themselves. Twenty years ago she began her training as a Biblical Life Coach in order to better help her clients cope with the difficulties life threw at them.

Women care about beauty. In fact, it is the core of who they are. But not all women want to be fashionable or glamorous; some would much prefer a casual look. Catrina has a way of helping women understand themselves so that they can be themselves, glamorous or not.

Over the years she has developed a system to offer image assessments in professional, party or retreat settings. She calls these events Supreme MakeOvers (or SMOs). During a SMO, she helps women identify and understand their personal Image Identity (Img.ID) and teaches them guidelines for accentuating their individual style. But her focus is more on the heart than it is on the image, because a makeover will wear off. Confidence should not. The key to true and lasting confidence is knowing who you are as well as Whose you are.

As a motivational speaker Catrina is a personal development pioneer. She has a unique way of intertwining fashion and faith into a beautiful balance. If you would like to learn more, or are interested in having Catrina speak at your event, contact her at www.catrinawelch.com.

Catrina has written a number of other books, including *Know Who You Are: Guidelines for Your Personal Image Identity,* and *Supreme MakeOver: a Rich and Refreshing Devotional Experience.* Find them on her website. She is the founder of Confident Beauty Ministries on Cape Cod, where she resides with her husband and children.